# GETTING IN FRONT ON DATA

## Who Does What

first edition

## Thomas C. Redman, Ph.D.

### "the Data Doc"

Published by:

2 Lindsley Road
Basking Ridge, NJ 07920 USA

https://www.TechnicsPub.com

Cover design by John Fiorentino
Edited by Alex Nuti-de Biasi

ISBN, print ed.       9781634621267
ISBN, Kindle ed.      9781634621274
ISBN, ePub ed.        9781634621281
ISBN, PDF ed.         9781634621298

First Printing 2016

Library of Congress Control Number: 2016943350

*For Nancy; our adventures continue.*

# TABLE OF CONTENTS

# FOREWORD
## By Thomas H. Davenport

There is little doubt that the importance of data to our economy and society has increased markedly over the last couple of decades. We now buy many things on the basis of data, treat medical conditions by data, run our financial system on data, socialize on data, and even run much of our government on data. Products and services increasingly revolve around data. We are so dependent upon data that we agonize about how much of our personal and organizational data leaks out to those who shouldn't have it.

As a result, interest in how to capitalize on data is at an all-time high. There are many books, conferences, and consulting practices on how to manage "big data" or create analytics from it. Vendors and their customers are increasingly focused on making sense of data, formulating predictions from it, and even converting it into automated recommendations and decisions. In short, dealing with "all things data" is a hallmark of the contemporary era.

Well, not all things. As Tom Redman points out, we seem to have left the topic of data quality behind. Most organizations have made little progress on this issue over the past couple of decades, and confront the problems it creates at every turn. It is as if a sports team devoted all of its energies and focus to offense—scoring points with data—with no orientation to defense, or preventing data-oriented problems. Redman admits that data quality may not be the sexiest aspect of data, but it is certainly among the most important. Without it, the transactions, analyses, recommendations, and decisions made on data are of little value.

Part of the value of this book, then, is simply convincing non-IT professionals of the value of data quality. Redman does that in a variety of ways in the early chapters, from example to metaphor. For many readers who are senior executives, this is worth the price of admission. They can decide that the problem is important enough to do something about it, and commission a concerted effort to address data quality.

Other readers, however, will be the ones charged with doing something about data quality, and they're in good hands as well with this book. Redman resists the common tendency to reduce data quality—or almost any data management problem—to an engineering exercise. Companies have been trying to engineer— draw diagrams, create abstract models, establish policies—their way around data problems for up to thirty or forty years by now. Few have anything to show for it.

Instead of engineering, Redman realized in his data quality work with companies that people were both the cause of and the solution to data quality problems. Instead of advocating for abstract data architectures, he argues for very tangible organizational architectures. Since he knows that data quality issues are inextricably bound with business processes and organizational structures, he also knows that to address those problems, you have to work with the people who own those processes and structures.

You may have already guessed that this is not simply an IT problem. Redman makes clear from the beginning of the book that data quality is an overall business problem, and can't be delegated to the IT organization. Since they don't own the relevant processes and structures, they are generally neither responsible for creating data quality problems nor able to fix them. There are, of course, technologies that can assist with identifying and solving data quality issues, but their power pales in comparison to the human capabilities in organizations.

It's time to stop reading this Foreword and jump into the real book. Do not hesitate; Redman makes it easy to engage with the issue. There is nothing that will prove too complex or technical for an adult person with a modicum of experience to understand. In other words, you have no excuses not to delve into this book and the issue of data quality in general. You and your organization will both be glad that you did.

Thomas H. Davenport

President's Distinguished Professor of IT and Management, Babson College

Research Fellow, MIT Initiative on the Digital Economy

Senior Advisor, Deloitte Analytics

Author of *Competing on Analytics*, *Big Data @ Work*, and *Only Humans Need Apply*

# ACKNOWLEDGEMENTS

If you measure success by the opportunity to work on something new and important, with courageous, smart, and caring people, then no one has been more successful than me. I started work on data quality at the great Bell Labs and AT&T before most knew what it was and long before anyone knew how important it would turn out to be. We sorted out some fundamental points and proved that "getting in front" is the superior approach to data quality, setting a path for others. Plenty of companies had the same problem, but none the vision of Bell Labs.

It's been my pleasure and privilege to work with thousands of great people since then. Among them are a few "provocateurs," those first to take up the "getting in front" approach in their industries and companies and prove its efficacy. If Bell Labs and AT&T created a path, the provocateurs helped pave it. All who follow are in their debt. While this path is certainly not easy—indeed many find it counterintuitive—the basic approaches, methods, tools, and benefits are available to all.

To continue the analogy, my goal with *Getting in Front on Data: Who Does What* is to illuminate the path, especially where the trail begins. Think of each instruction as a lamppost. Hundreds of people have contributed in some way or other. I thank them all.

I'm gratified to see a cadre of younger people replacing graybeards like me, as data only grows more pervasive and more important. Social media and smart, connected devices are but two examples. I expect recent generations to widen the path into a superhighway, paving it, making it smoother and faster.

I don't like the seemingly required "naming of names" in Acknowledgements. I've already noted that hundreds, maybe thousands, of people have contributed and I'm bound to leave someone out. But the thing that bothers me is that naming everyone obscures the biggest contributors, who don't get the full credit they deserve. So, the risk of offense aside, the following have most impacted my own thinking and practice: Bob Pautke, the first data quality provocateur; Jeff MacMillan, the first provocateur outside AT&T; Nikki Chang; Sarah Cliffe; Karl Fleischmann; John Fleming; Steve Hassmann; Liz Kirscher; Arnold Lent; Anany Levitin; Dennis Parton; and Lwanga Yonke.

Jennifer Daniels pushed me hard to make this the most concise and powerful book I could. Wow, was she tough! Tadhg Nagle, Bob Pautke, Dave Sammon, and Ken Self read early drafts and offered support. Andy O'Connell helped organize the material and sharpen it.

Next, my children and, later, their spouses and, still later, their children, have endured, usually with good humor, thousands of little experiments as I tried to understand how data quality management applied to family life.

Finally, Nancy. I'll never know why she cast her lot with a dreary statistician-in-training. But she's stood shoulder-to-shoulder with me for 40 years. I'm dead-certain my life is better because of her. I hope she feels the same way about me though I'm considerably less certain of that!

# INTRODUCTION

It has been eight years since my last book and over 15 since I devoted one wholly to data quality. A lot has happened since then – all things data, including big data; the "internet of things" data-driven cultures; advanced analytics; and chief data officers are penetrating every nook and cranny of every industry, company, department, and job. It's an exciting time!

Much of my work continues to address data quality, perhaps the least sexy topic in the data space. But it is, in my humble opinion, the most important for two reasons.

First, improving data quality presents an immediate opportunity to free up cash and people for longer-term investments. Companies waste enormous amounts of money, most of it hidden, dealing with bad data. While estimates vary enormously, take 20 percent of revenue or 50 percent of day-in, day-out costs as a starting point. Companies that make diligent efforts to improve data can reduce such costs by up to 80 percent.

Continuing in this vein, leaders and managers can better run their companies and departments when they have data they can trust. Managing a company or department is difficult under the best of circumstances and, quite

> I suspect that such savings are available to government agencies, nonprofits, scientific communities, and others but I've had less experience with them. Similarly, better data keeps us safer, advances equality, leads to better health care at lower cost, and on and on.

frankly, I don't know how many executives do it today without trustworthy, complete, and comprehensive data.

Second, bad data stands in the way of building a better future in data. Just as dirty fuel slows, even grounds, a supersonic jet, bad data stymies its full use and thereby prevents companies from gaining a competitive advantage. The disruption Uber brought to the taxi business, simply by connecting two pieces of data ("I'm looking for a ride" and "I'm looking for a fare"), should serve as a loud, clear message that data sparks whole new businesses. But many organizations find it difficult, even impossible, to take the right steps to improve data quality. One of the biggest obstacles is a persistent belief that responsibility for quality should reside with the tech department–"If it's in the computer, it must be IT's responsibility." Misconceptions like this one make a company unfit for data.

Companies must first address data quality if they are to find their futures. Hence, my title, *Getting In Front on Data*.

I help companies become fit for data by getting the right people, structures, and cultures in place. More specifically, I help leaders and provocateurs (a term I'll explore more fully below) see the benefits, gain experience, and build the capabilities they need. Those experiences formed the basis of an article, "Data's Credibility Problem," that I wrote for *Harvard Business Review* in 2013. This book expands on that piece, resynthesizing my ideas and pulling together my work with clients (including some truly transformative successes and more than a few failures) over the past 30 years.

Improving data quality means getting in front on the issues that cause bad data. I hope that sounds obvious—this approach is my second motivation for my title. Obvious as it may appear, too many companies haven't done what it takes to make it happen. This is too bad. After all, eliminating a single root cause may prevent tens of thousands of errors. Get the right people in the right roles and this happens quickly!

I've written this book with three specific audiences in mind:

- *Senior executives.* I hope to turn them on to data quality, guide them on building needed organizational capabilities, and help them understand the specific actions they can take. There are enormous gains to be had, but these gains have to be seized!

- *Those charged with leading the data quality effort.* My goal is to help these leaders orient their efforts more incisively.
- *Anyone who touches data in his or her job.* That is just about everyone. After all, get the data you need and all goes well. Don't get what you need and the job is far tougher! We have to make corrections, look for other sources, and sometimes even guess. In this respect, data quality is personal. We should all treat it as such!

Frankly, most of us are way too tolerant of bad data. This may be the most important reason that a solvable problem persists. It is time to demand better, to step up to our roles as data customers, clarify what we need most, and take steps to get it. It is also time to recognize that the data we create impacts the next person in line – our customers. We need to do a better job for them as well.

Thus, these roles as *data customers* and *data creators*, which we all play every day, are essential. I hope a light bulb goes off and we say to ourselves, "Yes of course I'm a data customer and yes of course I am a data creator!"

While these roles are at once obvious, they are also revolutionary. Getting started is a challenge, requiring provocateurs, who provoke the organization to get in front on data. My fondest hope is that this book unleashes the provocateur in all of us.

But of course, it is not enough that a few people get it. These roles must be driven across the entire work team, department, and company. That takes *leaders, data quality teams, embedded data managers,* people I call *data maestros,* with broad and deep expertise, and a specialist *chief data architect.* It also requires outstanding tech support.

I've studied the organic nature of data in organizations for a good long while. With the right people in the right spots, quality improves quickly. Done properly, getting in front on data is beautiful, even elegant. I hope more people come to appreciate this.

At the same time, I'm fully aware that people have less time to study. So I've crafted *Getting in Front on Data* as an instruction book and directed chapters toward specific roles. No matter who you are, you'll find explicit instructions in here.

I've also kept it as concise as possible. Data quality issues come in dozens of forms, but I'll focus on two that bedevil almost everyone. "The data is wrong" is the most common. "I don't understand what the data means", the second issue, is a bit more subtle. A classic example involves NASA losing a Martian lander because engineers confused English and metric units.[1] Closer to home, almost all companies complain that their "systems don't talk to each other," a direct result of the lack of clarity in data definition.

My plan for this book is as follows:

Chapter 1 synthesizes the why, who, how, and when.

Chapter 2 is an unabashed "What's in it for me?" First, it describes some simple tools to help develop a "case for improvement" at the work team, department, and company levels. Second, it describes the almost irresistible dynamic that causes people and companies to approach data quality the wrong way.

Then Chapters 3 through 8 consider the various data quality roles in turn. Chapter 3 focuses on customers, most of whom, as I've noted, have been way too tolerant of bad data for way too long.

Chapter 4, for data creators, consists of two parts. The first part covers "must-dos" for all creators; the second views data creation in the context of process management, an extremely powerful framework and organizing paradigm than more companies should employ.

---

[1] "Orbiter Lost Because NASA Forgot Metrics," *Asbury Park Press*, October 1, 1999.

Chapters 5 through 8 focus on provocateurs, data quality teams, senior leaders, and technologists, respectively.

Along the way, I've provided organization charts to help leaders understand the roles and people they need to put in place.

Chapter 9 presents two case studies in great depth. One features AT&T's work to address the "this data is wrong" issue and the other examines Aera Energy's efforts on the "I don't understand what the data means" issue.

All of this may appear overwhelming. So Chapter 10, "Advancing Data Quality," calls out a few important instructions for everyone. It also urges readers and their companies to get on with it.

This book will not cover every situation. In keeping the focus narrow, I leave it to readers to extend the getting in front approach to other situations. That said, two circumstances demand attention:

- Those faced by decision makers and data scientists when demand for quality is high and time is short.
- Automated measurement, connected devices, and the Internet of Things (IoT).

Appendices aim squarely at these.

Further, details and nuance abound. A more senior provocateur has wider latitude than a lower-level one. You'll emphasize some things when your primary customer is internal and others when it is a paying customer. Finally, good data quality programs mirror their corporate cultures. For example, some companies have the discipline to tackle big, complicated improvement opportunities; others need to break them down into a series of smaller efforts.

So see yourself in these roles. Then dive in. Interpret the instructions in ways that best suit your circumstances and strengths. Have fun, and good luck!

# CHAPTER 1
## Data Quality: Why, How, Who, and When?

## WHY?

Recently a media executive asked me to put data quality in everyday language. "Did you trust the data you used to make your most recent decision of real importance?" I asked him.

"No," he replied. "I did not. In fact, I can't recall a time when I fully trusted the data. I view it as my job to make the best call, even recognizing there are problems with the quality."

He's not alone. In a recent survey conducted by *Harvard Business Review*, only 16 percent of managers expressed strong confidence in the accuracy of the data underlying their business decisions.[2]

Further, the media executive's comments betray a simple reality for almost everyone: they must do their work in spite of bad data. A geologist in an oil company can't trust reports about existing wells; a salesperson can't trust the contact leads she has been given; a back office worker in a financial services company can detect details about a municipal bond that are inaccurate; a shipping clerk spends more time dealing with returned parcels than sending out new ones. It's a problem for individuals and work teams, up and down the organization; for departments and entire companies; in the private sector and the public sector.

---

[2] See "Data and Organizational Issues Reduce Confidence," http://www.redmond.es/descargas/WP-HBR-Pulse-Survey-EN.pdf. The survey was conducted in August 2013 by Harvard Business Review Analytic Services.

Quite naturally, all do their best in the face of bad data—correcting errors, searching for other sources, sorting out what the data means, and otherwise working around the inaccuracies. But they don't always succeed and bad data goes on to the next person, process, or application.

Many errors cause only minor problems—a package is sent to the wrong address, an interest payment is too big, an employee gets more than his allotted vacation, and so on. A few lead to "train wrecks," such as the aforementioned Martian lander or death following the transplant of an organ carrying the wrong blood type. Indeed, examples of bad data and its impact make national and international news with disturbing frequency.[3]

The damage doesn't stop there. Bad decisions are made based on bad data. Customers get angry, bosses frustrated, and internal rancor is sewn. One of the biggest political fights I've witnessed involved "whose data was better" and the disputing parties didn't speak to each other for months after.

Finally, bad data is like a virus. There is no telling where it will show up or the damage it will do.[4] Falsified data on mortgage applications in the run-up to the financial crisis provides a perfect example. The immediate consequence was that people took out mortgages they couldn't pay off. Bad as this was, the damage could have been contained; but these mortgages were repackaged into more complex financial products, amplifying the risk and eventually failing in a spectacular way.

---

[3] I included "The Dirty Dozen" of 12 data quality train wrecks in *Data Driven, Profiting from Your Most Important Business Asset*, Harvard Business Press, 2008. Articles from the *New York Times* that caught my eye in March 2016 involve psychology studies (Benedict Carey, "Report Questioning Psychology Studies is Criticized," March 4), Chinese growth statistics (Edward Wong, "Facing Skepticism on its Data, China Adjusts Growth Target," March 5) blood testing (Katie Thomas, "Blood Tests Questioned, But Device is Still in Use," March 18), Theranos, (Andrew Pollack, "Study of Theranos Medical Tests Finds Irregular Results," March 28), and Valeant's accounting (Peter Eaves, "Valeant's Small Accounting Error is a Warning Signal to Investors of Bigger Problems," March 29). Issues rooted in bad data make the national and international news every day.

[4] From 1988 to 1995 I led the data quality lab at AT&T Bell Laboratories. This observation stems from that period, though I do not recall who said it first.

*Thus, the first and most immediate reason to improve data quality is to improve current business performance.*

Now let's look ahead. It is now trite to observe that data already plays vital and growing roles in all companies. Indeed, data dominates entire industries. Health care runs on data. Other than cash transactions, the finance sector consists of nothing but data. Logistics depend on data—indeed, half the value in delivering a shipping container around the world lies in the data.[5]

Further, many have opined that data is "the new oil." Just as it took oil to power the machines of the Industrial Age, so it takes data to power tomorrow's technologies, products, companies, and economies.

For example, some managers labor to create data-driven cultures, essentially bringing more and more data to the decision-making table, and so improving everything little by little. Other companies are using big data and advanced analytics to innovate, and find and leverage insights to make better products and processes. Uber has informationalized the taxi business—just one example of the new business opportunities in data. More and more, data is key to competing effectively.

At the same time, it is clear enough that you can't compete using bad data: You can't expect people to become data-driven when they don't trust the data; even the most sophisticated analysis is no better than the data on which it is based; and exposing bad data in markets is risky. Departments and companies that hope to build a future in data simply must improve. Finally, though not the original objective, many find getting in front on data quality "transformative," re-arranging the ways people think about their jobs, changing relationships, and helping create that future.

*Thus, the second, and possibly more important, reason to improve quality is that you can't build a future in data without doing so.*

---

[5] Stewart Taggart, "The 20-Ton Packet," Wired.com, October 1999, www.wired.com/ 1999/10/ports/.

## HOW AND WHO?

Data quality pioneers have made tremendous progress in the last 25 years or so, working out the basic philosophies, approaches, methods, and organizational structures needed to "get in front on data quality." They essentially created the most important data correctly, the first time, thus doing away with all that added work.

Getting in front works far better than one might reasonably expect. Companies across a range of industries, including telecom, financial services, oil and gas, and data providers, have made and sustained order of magnitude improvements.

The benefits have also proven enormous, again far greater than one might expect. Those whose goal was saving money have reduced expenses by hundreds of millions. Those less concerned with saving money and more concerned with better decision-making, improved customer satisfaction, or more competitive positioning, have achieved these goals.

Until you get the hang of it, getting in front seems odd. It represents new thinking, requires people to take new roles, and features some new management tools (and a few technical ones). But there is no deep mystery.

### A database is like a lake

To fully appreciate the common sense of getting in front, consider Figure 1.1. In the analogy, a lake is likened to a database, the lake water to the data, and the stream to a business process that feeds new data into the database. If there is pollution in the stream, it feeds polluted water into the lake and, if people drink from it, they're going to get sick.

There are three ways to deal with a polluted lake:

- Focus your efforts on those who get sick–get good at quickly identifying them and develop efficient systems for taking them to the hospital, pumping their stomachs, and supporting their recoveries.

- Clean the water before people drink it.
- Find and eliminate the sources of pollutants, so that only clean water will flow into the lake.

Figure 1.1 A database is like a lake.

For data quality, the choices are just as stark:

- Let those who use the data fend for themselves and deal with the consequences.
- Find and fix data errors before people use it.
- Get in front by creating data correctly the first time. This means finding and eliminating the root causes of error.

Getting in front depends on *data creators*, including anyone who fills in a form, populates a database, crafts a management report, or makes a decision, and those responsible for devices such as thermostats and blood

In part, getting in front works due to two observations:

1. It is always easier to create data correctly than it is to find errors and correct them.
2. It usually costs no more to create correct data than incorrect data.

monitoring equipment. In this respect, practically everyone is a data creator! Still, it is usually more appropriate to think of processes, work teams, departments, and companies, rather than people, as data creators and customers. This is certainly the case for complex data products, financial reports, and sophisticated analyses.

### Connecting data customers and creators

But as powerful as the lake analogy is, it does not point out which data is most important. That's where *data customers* come in – their needs drive what's *most important*. As used here, a customer is anyone who uses data in any way. Again, practically everyone is a data customer! Finally, it is often most appropriate to view operational, analytic, decision-making, and planning processes as data customers.

Unfortunately most data customers, in the pressures of day-in, day-out work, attempt to find and correct errors (e.g., clean the lake) rather than communicating their needs to data creators. It simply doesn't occur to them that they should look upstream, clarify their needs, and help the creators do a better job. For their parts, data creators see no reason to do anything different. So they continue to produce bad data.

> I wish to be careful here. I am not suggesting that people shouldn't correct erroneous data before they use it. Using data you know is bad or passing it on is simply irresponsible. At the same time, it is equally irresponsible to continue such corrections, day-in and day-out, without attempting to get in front of the problem.

To get in front, creators and customers must talk. When customers articulate their most important needs, almost all data creators strive to meet those needs and quality improves rapidly.

A watershed moment occurs when people realize that they are *both data customers and data creators*. And just as they must work with creators in their roles as customers, so too must they work with their customers, the next department, bosses, corporate customers, the public, regulators, and so on, in their roles as creators.

Of course, life is more complicated than this. While these basic roles are seemingly obvious, they don't appear out of thin air. A data customer may need data created months before, and three departments removed. The data creator may not know who uses what he or she creates. Both may feel trapped in organizational silos that make communication difficult.

That's where data quality management comes in. Its main job is to help connect data creators and customers, facilitating direct communications between the two. This may also mean providing measurements to help identify sources of errors, training creators on improvement and control, actively managing change, engaging more senior management, and lending expertise to help solve some particularly nettlesome problems.

Powerful, professional data quality teams should include "embedded data managers," who are placed in the line, as close to data customers and data creators as possible to help data creators and customers fulfill their responsibilities. Embedded data managers also help data creators and data customers see new opportunities in data and unlock their potential.

### Two moments that matter[6]

The focus on customers and creators and the need for them to connect is so important that I wish to motivate it in a different way. To do so, follow a piece of data around. Only two moments in its entire lifetime truly matter. The first is its moment of creation. After being generated, often in the blink of an eye, it may be moved from place to place, stored in databases, combined with other data, transformed slightly and stored in a data warehouse. Most of the time, it just sits there, leading an incredibly boring existence.

---

[6] See http://dataqualitysolutions.com/video-learning/ for a short video on the subject.

If the data is lucky, it experiences another moment that matters: Someone uses it– to complete an operation, as part of an analysis, to make a decision, to craft a

> Of course the vast majority of data never experiences that moment of use. At most a few percent of data qualify as "most important."

plan, or to do something else. Quality is determined at that moment – the data is either fit for use, relevant, accurate, and well-defined, according to the customer's needs, or it is not. Note though, that how well the moment of use goes is set at the moment of creation. Created properly and the moment of use should go well. Created improperly and the moment of use will not go well.

Thus, from a quality perspective, the only two moments that truly matter are the moment of creation and the moment of use. It follows that we must direct as much attention as we can to these moments—that customers and creators must do all they can to ensure those moments go well! It also follows that we must connect these moments. While customers and creators sometimes find each other, active, engaged data quality management ensures it happens at scale, for all of the most important data.

### Getting started

While the roles for data creators, data customers, and quality managers are simple, powerful, and almost obvious, they also require a huge change in thinking and approach. Most creators have no idea that their data causes such pain. Customers tend to fend for themselves, and quality management is sidelined and ignored.

It takes a special spark to transition from the status quo to getting in front. That spark occurs when someone becomes so dissatisfied they scream to themselves, "There has to be a better way!" They display the courage to give getting in front a try. I call these people

> To be clear, provocateurs are not usually motivated by data quality per se. Rather, they want to solve a business problem and bad data is getting in the way. Thus improved data is the means to achieve an objective, not the objective itself.

*provocateurs* and they usually aren't data experts. They may be executives, middle managers, data scientists or industry specialists, clerks, even entry-level employees. The only requirements are an unwillingness to accept bad data and the courage to try something new.

Spurred on by their frustration, provocateurs typically have an enormous impact within their immediate spans of control. But they cannot change entire companies on their own. If the good efforts are to go further, more senior management (dare I say leadership) must take over.

People frequently complain to me that their senior managers "don't get data quality." My own experience is somewhat different. True, they don't think much about data quality, but after just a few minutes of discussion, they get it just fine. The larger problem is that they don't know what they personally should do about it.

As I'll make clear, the organization's top leaders must insist that their departments and companies adopt the getting in front approach, build the roles described here into the structure of their organizations, focus the effort, and advance a culture that values data.

### Let tech do tech!

I haven't said a word, until now, about technologists. That's deliberate. Too many data programs make the mistake of putting technology first. Although technologists can do many wondrous things in supporting data quality, scaling up data programs, and bringing down costs, they have proven to be ineffective leaders of data quality efforts.

Tech cannot set objectives, select and build support for the right approach, put the right people in place, or sort out what is most important. Nor can it save a data quality program that ignores these factors.

Instead, I find it extremely helpful to approach business problems and opportunities in the following left-to-right fashion, with tech last:[7]

    1. Goal/Approach → 2. Organization → 3. Process → 4. Technology

This aligns with the way corporate leaders think about the business. They realize they bear ultimate responsibility for results and know they have to have the right people, structure, governance, and culture in place to achieve them. Interestingly, positioning tech last also increases its chance of success. Rather than selling an initiative, tech focuses on what it does best—using technology to increase scale and decrease unit cost.

## WHEN?

To oversimplify a bit, a data quality program typically unfolds in three phases (refer to Figure 1.2):

- **Getting traction**, during which a provocateur tries the get in front of data approach as a means to solve a specific problem;
- **Achieving real results**, in which data creators, data customers, quality managers, and embedded data managers work in concert to make significant improvements and put in place a sustaining data quality program on a small scale; and
- **Going to the next level**, in which the data quality program, rather than plateauing (as many do), grows beyond the provocateur's reach, to an entire department or the company as a whole. Senior leadership is essential.

Transitioning from a "provocateur-led" to a "senior management-led" data program is a big deal. Just as data creators and customers had to learn new roles,

---

[7] I've drawn on many sources in developing this process. John Roberts, *The Modern Firm Organizational Design for Performance and Growth*, Oxford University Press, 2004 has had enormous impact on my thinking here.

so too does senior management. Teaching them falls to either provocateurs or (more usually) data quality management. Since data quality programs go as far and as fast as demanded by the senior leader perceived to be leading the effort, I cannot emphasize this enough!

Figure 1.2 A provocateur stimulates a data quality effort, gaining traction and achieving real results. But the effort plateaus and leadership is needed to move the program "to the next level."

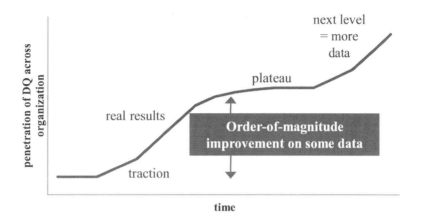

## IN SUMMARY

*Getting in front on data quality* means creating the most important data correctly, the first time. For this to happen, people (and processes) must step up to their responsibilities as data creators and data customers. When both make reasonable efforts to connect, to focus on customers' most important needs, and to find and eliminate root causes of error, data quality improves rapidly. Data creators and data customers thus play the most important roles. And all of us play these roles, every day!

Data quality management helps make creators and customers effective, by helping them connect, supporting embedded data managers, and being the day-in, day-out face of the effort. Technologists help make others more efficient. Once the basic processes work, automation increases scale and decreases unit cost.

Getting started is tough. It takes a special person, whom I call a provocateur, to challenge the status quo and give the give getting in front approach a try. And not long thereafter, senior leaders must take the mantle and extend the effort to everyone!

Bad data is an equal opportunity peril, adding cost, making it more difficult to run things, and compromising decisions. It angers customers, adds risk that those interesting insights discovered by an analytics effort aren't so, and generally stymies any effort that depends on data. Still, most people must develop a deeper understanding of how they, their work teams, departments, and companies are directly affected before they get involved. This chapter helps do just that, outlining exercises to baseline current quality levels, estimate costs, and synthesize an overall motivation or justification. Just as important, the chapter explores why so many people attack data quality the wrong way, operating what I call "hidden data factories," rather than getting in front.

Over the years there have been many high-level studies of the costs associated with bad data. Our work at Bell Labs in the 1990s led me to conclude that about half of the cost in a service department was spent accommodating bad data. A 2002 TDWI study put the cost of bad customer data alone at $600B/year; and a 2016 IBM graphic puts the cost at $3.1T/year in the U.S., which is about 20 percent of the Gross Domestic Product. Finally, bad data is behind the scenes in stories of national and international importance every day. While the examples and numbers stun, few people take them as a call to arms because they don't see how they are personally impacted. Hence my focus here on "what's in it for me."[8]

---

[8] Citations for the callout bubble above: Thomas C. Redman, "The Impact of Poor Data Quality on the Typical Enterprise," *Communications of the ACM, Volume 41*, No 2, February, 1998; Wayne Eckerson, *Data Quality and the Bottom Line: Achieving Business Success Though a Commitment to High-Quality Data*, The Data Warehousing Report Series, 2002, Seattle, WA; http://www.ibmbigdatahub.com/ infographic/four-vs-big-data.

**Instructions:**

1. Estimate current data quality levels, using the Friday Afternoon Measurement.
2. Recognize your hidden data factories for what they are—poor, expensive alternatives to getting in front on data quality.
3. Estimate the non-value-added costs associated with these hidden data factories.
4. Identify hard-to-quantify costs of special importance.
5. Think through long-term implications.
6. Assemble the motivation/justification/business case for getting in front.

## Do I Have a Data Quality Problem?

**Use the Friday Afternoon Measurement to estimate your error rate**

Invest a few hours to make a Friday Afternoon Measurement (FAM)[9] and answer the question "Do I have a data quality problem?" Figure 2.1, below, presents the protocol for doing so.

Figure 2.1 Protocol (i.e., steps) for the Friday Afternoon Measurement.

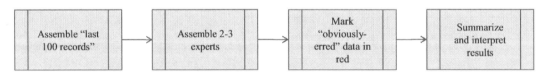

---

[9] I designed the FAM in response to the need for companies to make a simple, defensible measurement of data quality without investing much time or money. I call it the FAM because many people can fit it in on a Friday afternoon, as the pace of work slows and most think only about their weekends. See http://dataqualitysolutions.com/video-learning/ for a short video.

First, assemble a spreadsheet that looks much like Figure 2.2. Take the last 100 data records that you used, created, or processed, limiting yourself to the 10 to 15 most essential attributes (or fields, columns, or elements).

Figure 2.2 Step 1 of the Friday Afternoon Measurement Protocol.

|  | Attribute 1: Name | Attribute 2: Size | Attribute 3: Amount | Etc. (for the 10-15 most important attributes) |
|---|---|---|---|---|
| Record A | Jane Doe | Null | $472.13 | |
| Record B | John Smith | Medium | $126.93 | |
| Record C | Stuart Madnick | XXXL | Null | |
| Record D | Thoams Jones | | | |
| | | | | |
| | | | | |
| Record 100 | James Olsen | One Locked Place | $76.24 | |

Step 2 is to gather two to three people who understand the data intimately. Invite them to a two-hour meeting. Step 3 calls for those experts to mark the obviously erred data in red (the dark shaded cells), producing a spreadsheet like that in Figure 2.3.

Figure 2.3 Step 3 of the Friday Afternoon Measurement Protocol.

|  | Attribute 1: Name | Attribute 2: Size | Attribute 3: Amount | Etc. (for the 10-15 most important attributes) |
|---|---|---|---|---|
| Record A | Jane Doe | Null | $472.13 | |
| Record B | John Smith | Medium | $126.93 | |
| Record C | Stuart Madnick | XXXL | Null | |
| Record D | Thoams Jones | | | |
| | | | | |
| | | | | |
| Record 100 | James Olsen | One Locked Place | $76.24 | |

Step 4 is to summarize and interpret the results. To do so, rate each record as "perfect" if there is no red in its row and "not perfect" otherwise. Next, count the errors for each attribute and total the number of perfect records. The spreadsheet in Figure 2.4 shows the results.

> The Friday Afternoon Measurement works because it is usually easy for those well-versed in the nuances of the data to spot most errors.

Figure 2.4 Step 4 of the Friday Afternoon Measurement Protocol.

| | Attribute 1: Name | Attribute 2: Size | Attribute 3: Amount | Etc. | Record perfect? (y/n) |
|---|---|---|---|---|---|
| Record A | Jane Doe | Null | $472.13 | | n |
| Record B | John Smith | Medium | $126.93 | | y |
| Record C | Stuart Madnick | XXXL | Null | | n |
| Record D | Thoams Jones | | | | n |
| | | | | | |
| | | | | | |
| Record 100 | James Olsen | One Locked Place | $76.24 | | n |
| N of errors | 4 | 25 | 9 | Count perfect | 67 |

In this case, the data "passed" 67 times out of 100. Said differently, Data Quality (DQ) =.67 (indicated in the lower right shaded cell in the spreadsheet). This means that a full one-third of the records you need are not fit for use. You do indeed have a problem and almost certainly a big one.

> There are many subtleties built into the step-by-step instructions for the FAM. One involves requiring that all attributes be correct. It stems from the observation that if even one attribute is erred, the customer can't use the data record without correction.

To calibrate, I've seen FAM and other initial results as low as DQ =.08 and as high as DQ =.95. In a recent Dun and Bradstreet report on business-to-business marketing data quality, scores came in between DQ = .13 and .23 (though these numbers are not fully comparable).[10] For FAM, most score between .30 and .80. So DQ = .67 is on the high end of typical.

A second FAM subtlety involves taking the *last* 100 data records, which aims to eliminate a tough inferential issue. In reporting results, don't try to generalize. Simply state that "in the last 100 records, 33 failed."

Almost everyone is surprised, even shocked, by their low scores. And this emotional energy can help turn them into provocateurs!

Conversely, I've never heard anyone say, "Excellent. I feared things were much worse!"

## THE WRONG REACTION IN THE FACE OF BAD DATA

Almost everyone, from the shipping clerk trying to get a package to the right address, to the mid-level executive trying to manage his budget, to the data scientist trying to make sure her analyses don't go awry, to the senior leader trying to set strategic direction, do their best to deal with bad data. Many, almost unconsciously, go to extraordinary lengths in doing so. But are they doing the right things?

Consider Samantha, a rising star executive, preparing for her first meeting with the Board. While reviewing her presentation, she and her assistant Steve notice something that looks strange in the sales numbers from the Widget Department. After some discussion, she asks him to research the numbers. An hour later he's found the problem, explained the corrected number to her, and updated the presentation.

And off Samantha goes. She connects with the Board, and there is a good discussion around the very number that her assistant corrected. She returns to her

---

[10] See *The B2B Marketing Data Report 2016*, Dun and Bradstreet, http://www.dnb.com/marketing/media/state-of-marketing-data-2016.html and Shelly Lucas, "What's with the Mellow Attitude to Data Quality," http://www.dnb.com/perspectives/marketing-sales/mellow-attitude-towards-data-quality.html.

office elated. She thanks Steve, gives him an on-the-spot bonus of $200, and tells him to take the rest of the day off.

As he's leaving, she remarks, "You know, you should check the Widget Department's numbers every month. We were lucky this time. I don't want to risk it ever again!" Steve agrees and heads out the door.

### The Hidden Data Factory

It is easy to cheer their dedication, hard work, and fortune. But let's take a deeper look. In deciding to check the Widget Department's numbers on an ongoing basis, Samantha and Steve have set up what I call a "hidden data factory." They conduct extra work to search for and correct or otherwise accommodate bad data.

Note that Samantha didn't attempt to get in front of the issue. She could have called her peer, the head of the Widget Department, to advise him of the issue. She could have simply explained her requirements. She could have offered to lead an improvement project to get to the bottom of the issue. She could have taken steps to correct the corporate numbers, rather than leaving others to be victimized. Subtly perhaps, in setting up her own little hidden data factory, she has assumed responsibility for the quality of Widget Department numbers, even though she doesn't know the first thing about widgets. Who even knows if the number she presented to the Board was correct? And because the underlying business process is unchanged, the widget people continue to pump out more bad data, so the one-man hidden data factory (Steve) is doomed to go on forever.

> One could also argue that our rising star should be shown the door. Leaving others within one's company to be victimized is the height of managerial irresponsibility and is not acceptable. Ever.
>
> Whatever side you take, the vignette clearly illustrates a cultural aspect of data quality.

You can't blame Samantha for correcting numbers in advance of her important meeting. After all, it would be simply irresponsible to present bad numbers to the Board. At the same time, she elected, perhaps without thinking, not to get in front of future issues. Unfortunately, she is not alone. It is exactly this dynamic which leads to hidden data factories all over the company!

When you bust open a typical process, it looks something like Figure 2.5. Steps 1, 3, and 4 are the value-adding work–the process's raison d'être. Steps 2 and 5 constitute the hidden factory.

Figure 2.5 A typical business process features value-added work (Steps 1, 3, and 4) and non-value-added work (Steps 2 and 5) solely to address data quality issues.

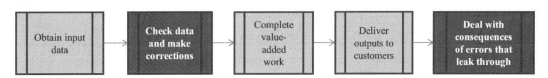

Hidden data factories abound at all levels and in all areas. They attest to the great value people, at all levels and in all departments, place on high-quality data. Many billing departments conceal hidden data factories. They can proliferate between departments, as sales wastes time dealing with error-filled prospect data received from marketing, and operations deals with flawed customer orders received from sales.

There's usually an enormous hidden data factory in IT to resolve discrepancies between the various HR, finance, inventory management, production, and other systems because key data definitions don't align. I've worked with companies that purchased the same data from several sources, compared the various versions, labeled the one they liked best the "golden copy," and used it going forward. Imagine being so rich that you could purchase several copies of anything and throw all but one away!

Hidden data factories abound in knowledge work as well. A geologist can't find the survey he needs and so orders another. Analysts spend inordinate time checking the facts before they do their analyses. When a finance manager can't square results from two sources, she has to figure out which (if either) is right. People from two departments may fight over whose numbers are better, which produces an oft-combustible data factory. And data scientists complain that they spend more time cleaning up data than analyzing it.

There are hidden data factories at the executive level as well. I've already noted the one set up by Samantha. In the same vein, many senior managers don't trust the numbers coming from the financial system and so maintain their own records. And some executives hedge monthly numbers in case something is missing.

### Better, faster, cheaper

The great Dr. Armand Feigenbaum[11] coined the term "hidden factory" during the quality revolution in manufacturing to describe work conducted by one person or group to accommodate the errors made by another. Hidden factories were shown as responsible for up to 40 percent of a manufacturing plant's costs and they led to other problems as well.

So too with hidden data factories:

- They add time. Identifying suspect data is time-consuming enough. Correcting it takes even longer.
- They add cost. I'll provide a simple calculator that provides a rough estimate just below.
- They don't work very well. I've already noted that finding and fixing errors is tough work and, even under the best of circumstances, too many errors leak through. Indeed, most hidden data factories are run in an ad hoc manner and under enormous time pressure.
- They provide a false sense of security, as the Samantha vignette attests.

Poor alternatives to getting in front indeed!

---

[11] See for example, Tim Stevens, "Dr. Armand Feigenbaum on the Cost of Quality and the Hidden Factory," July 4, 1994 http://www.industryweek.com/quality/dr-armand-feigenbaum-cost-quality-and-hidden-factory or "The Encyclopedia of Operations Management."

## USE THE RULE OF TEN TO ESTIMATE COSTS

Bad data does lots of damage, but it is incredibly difficult to pin down most of the associated costs. For example, no one knows how to calculate the cost of a bad decision. Even the most basic costs, those associated with the hidden data factory, are difficult to determine. After all, accounting systems are not designed to track them (one reason the factory remains hidden). Still, the so-called "Rule of Ten"[12] yields a quick and often good-enough estimate. It reflects the high costs associated with the non-value-adding steps of Figure 2.5 and states:

> It costs ten times as much to complete a unit of work when the data is erred as it does when it is perfect.

Now, suppose your work team must complete 100 units of work in a given period of time, and it costs a dollar to complete each unit when the data is perfect. Under these assumptions, the cost of the value-adding work is $100 (a dollar for each unit). The total cost in the face of errors and the cost associated with non-value-adding work depends on the fraction of those errors. If DQ = .67, as obtained from the FAM, then:

### Rule of Ten Calculator

| | | |
|---|---|---|
| The cost of the 67 perfect records | = 67 * $1 | = $67 |
| The cost of the 33 bad records | = 33 * $10 | = $330 |
| Total cost | | = $397 |
| **Cost of value-added work (from above)** | | **= $100** |
| **Cost of non-value-added work** | | **= $297** |

The conclusion is as follows: "For every dollar we spend on value-added data work, we spend three performing non-value-added work so we can use the data!"

While this estimate can't be defended in any scientific sense, it can help you start a conversation. Your colleagues may propose a multiplier other than ten that they

---

[12] See page 47 in *Data Driven*.

consider more appropriate. If so, simply redo the calculation. I've never heard anyone propose a multiplier less than five. Even at that level, the cost of the hidden data factory proves enormous. In the example above, the cost of non-value-added work is $132, still greater than the cost of the value-added work.

## IDENTIFY "HARD-TO-QUANTIFY" COSTS OF SPECIAL IMPORTANCE

I wish to re-emphasize that the costs associated with data factories do not capture all of the damage that stems from bad data. Indeed, it doesn't even reflect all of the added costs. Quite frequently other things, such as the added difficulties in running your department or company, angered customers, and the lack of trust in an analytic insight, are far more important!

Thus, look at the damage more holistically. Use the Cost of Poor Data Quality (CoPDQ) checklist, in Figure 2.6, simply noting which are of equal or greater importance than cost. The CoPDQ checklist lists frequent "hard-to-quantify" costs associated with bad data. In many cases, these are of greater importance than the added costs.

Figure 2.6 Other common costs associated with bad data.

1. Day-in, day-out management: More difficult to run the department/company.
2. Professional time wasted: Professionals (geologists, financial analysts, data scientists, etc.) are in short supply and spend too much time dealing with bad data.
3. Customers: Bad data angers customers, hurting sales and reputation.
4. Intra-Department work: Departments don't trust each other's data, making it more difficult to work together.
5. Decisions: Poorer and delayed decisions.
6. Big Data: People don't trust the results of Big Data analytics projects.
7. Time: Sometimes people have to move quickly and bad data slows them down.
8. Tech projects: Bad data increases the risk that large tech projects fail.
9. Security: Bad data makes it more difficult to tell the good guys from the bad guys.
10. Unwanted attention: Bad data leads to bad press and/or regulatory scrutiny.
11. Competition: Bad data makes it more difficult to compete.
12. Cost: Added costs include data factories, hidden or otherwise, redundant systems, systems that don't talk, and so forth.

## THINK LONGER-TERM

A few people in each department and company should also think about data quality longer-term. Despite the flurry of media attention data is receiving, not enough people are worrying specifically about quality. In particular, most companies are already, quite literally, competing with data. Not only do they use data internally, they expose enormous quantities of data to their prospects and customers (think product descriptions); to their suppliers (think specifications) and competitors; to financial markets and regulators (think annual reports); and so forth. Some of that data is bad and sometimes prospects, customers, and financial markets take their business elsewhere. No one who's placed an online order for in-store pick-up only to be told at the pick-up counter, "Nope, we haven't had any of those for days," ever completely forgives the frustration.

And data is only growing more important. In my last book, *Data Driven*, I enumerated a long list of ways to "put data to work" and summarized each one. Based on research since then, I now recognize four basic strategies[13] (with dozens of variants) for competing with data. And bad data stymies all.

1. *Be data-driven.*[14] The essence of this strategy is that everyone who comes to the decision-making table–whether they're alone at the table or surrounded by dozens of others–brings more and more data along, with the result that people combine the data with their intuitive business sense and thereby make better decisions.

But you can't expect people to bring data they don't trust to the decision-making table.

---

[13] Thomas Redman, "4 Business Models for the Data Age," May 20, 2015, https://hbr.org/2015/05/4-business-models-for-the-data-age.

[14] The term "data-driven" has entered the lexicon over the last several years. On the strength of *Data Driven: Profiting from Your Most Important Business Asset*, which I wrote in 2008, some give me credit for introducing the term, but it seems unlikely to me that no one had used it before then.

2. *Use big data and advanced analytics to innovate.* This is a strategy of finding clues in the data and leveraging them to create better products and processes. The promise is enormous. Big data is all the rage right now, but deeper analysis of smaller data will likely prove just as effective.

But bad data can send even the cleverest algorithm astray. Further, even if you find something interesting in the (dirty) data, it is more difficult to take full advantage.

3. *Content is king.* Companies gain an edge by providing new and better content to customers. There are many variations of this strategy, from selling content directly (think Morningstar), infomediating (Google), and informationalization (Uber).

But exposing bad data in marketplaces is risky. For example, it is hard to imagine much success for Uber if rides don't show up when promised.

4. *Become the low-cost data provider.* Scaling up the direct costs described above, it is not hard to see that bad data may account for half of operational expenses and a significant fraction of other expenses. Companies seeking to compete by offering the lowest prices may find improving data quality is the best way to lower their cost structures.

Quite obviously you can't do so without a singular focus on data quality.

## So What's in It for Me?

The discussion above helps quickly and powerfully baseline the current state. The promise of getting in front involves reducing the error rate by an order of magnitude and taking advantage. Assemble a "before and after" picture as your motivation/justification/business case for data quality, such as the example in Table 2.1.

Table 2.1 An example justification/motivation for a department-level data quality effort.

| | Current State | Desired State |
|---|---|---|
| **DQ Level** | Customer Data: DQ = 43 percent | DQ = 95 percent |
| | Technical Data: DQ = 57 percent | DQ = 96 percent |
| | Media Data: DQ = 72 percent | DQ = 97 percent |
| **Cost** | Ops team spends two-thirds of its time on DQ | Get this to 20 percent (will require some investment) |
| | Data scientist team spends 75 percent of its time on DQ | Get this to 20 percent (will require some investment) |
| **Other Near-Term Impacts** | Too many anecdotal decisions in running department | Greater confidence in day-in, day-out decisions |
| | Data scientists are tough to find and bad data contributes to dissatisfaction | Reduce turnover by 50 percent |
| **Long-Term Impact** | We don't have the needed base of support to leverage analytics | Discussions focus on our analyses, not problems in the data |

## IN SUMMARY

Virtually everyone needs high-quality data and they know it, but are blind to how good or bad it is and its impact. You need to make the current state visible and you need to clarify the problems you wish to resolve. There is no great mystery.

You also need to accept that in setting up a hidden data factory you have become part of the problem. Recognize this constitutes non-value-added work. To reduce it, you must get in front on data quality.

# CHAPTER 3
## Data Customers Must Speak Up

While I know of no hard facts to support this claim, it seems to me that the dominant reason so much data is bad is that people tolerate it. It's remarkable, even paradoxical, that people will insist on the delivery of a complex product or service in perfect working order, but they will accept simple billing errors.[15] Big corporations have large supply-chain management groups to ensure that their suppliers are up to spec, but their efforts don't extend to data. This must change.

Unless you make your needs known, you have no reasonable expectation of quality data. Further, over the years I've worked on hundreds of data quality issues and so far, data creators not knowing what data customers want has been a major factor in each. In some cases, it's far and away the dominant factor. Once the two sides sit down together, data creators might say, "Thanks for this. We never knew who used that data. The system wouldn't let us move forward without it, so we always filled it in. But frankly, we just guessed. Now that we know what you need, we can do a much better job."

> I've seen plenty of other contributing factors–inadequate staffing, woefully ill-designed processes, and truly horrific data dictionaries. Even then explaining customer needs is essential. And it produces the fastest results.

Data customers simply must grow intolerant of bad data and speak up.

---

[15] I'm proofing this chapter in early April 2016 with a long feature on John Oliver's HBO Show, *Last Week Tonight*, firmly in mind. It examined failures in credit reporting, going back nearly 20 years.

Becoming a good customer is increasingly important the more data you require or the more quickly you use data; as things speed up, there is simply less time to run through a hidden data factory to make corrections. It's also increasingly important as one moves up the management chain. As the issues and opportunities become murkier, you need even better data, from more diverse sources, synthesized in creative ways.[16]

Yet as you rise through the ranks, getting what you need may be more difficult. Consider "bad news." Let's face it; people hate to bring the boss bad news. They delay, hoping things will turn around. They concoct far-fetched rationalizations for why things are not so bad. They deflect blame. So a boss must be clear about what she wants, understand the range of sources depended upon, and know whether they can be trusted.

Being a good customer is also of increasing importance to statisticians, analysts, data scientists, and anyone trying to find hidden treasures in the data. An algorithm combing through data doesn't give a whit whether the data is correct. And it is completely indifferent to subtle differences in data definitions. So you can explore data to your heart's content without giving data quality a second thought. But without high-quality data, you can't do the real work, which involves understanding something new about the world and building that new understanding into a product or service.

**The instructions for becoming a good data customer are quite straightforward:**

1. Recognize that you are a data customer.
2. Communicate your needs.
3. Innovate in your use of data and encourage data creators to innovate.
4. Actively manage data suppliers.
5. Make data factories more effective and as small as possible.

---

[16] There are many articles on this subject. Two of my favorites are Peter Drucker, "The Information Executives Truly Need," *Harvard Business Review*, Jan.-Feb. 1995, https://hbr.org/1995/01/the-information-executives-truly-need and Davide Niolini, Maja Korica, and Keith Ruddle, "Staying in the Know," *MIT Sloan Management Review*, Summer 2015, http://sloanreview.mit.edu/ article/staying-in-the-know/.

6. Build the organizational capabilities needed to follow these instructions for all your important data.

This chapter considers each in turn.

## RECOGNIZE THAT YOU ARE A DATA CUSTOMER

The first step in every addiction program is "Admit you have a problem." For those not getting the high-quality data they need, that first step translates as becoming aware that you are a customer of data. And becoming a good one entails some hard work!

I use three definitions of data quality, depending on the circumstances. Two are especially pertinent in this chapter. My formal definition aligns closely with the near-term goal of improving business performance:[17]

> *Data is of high quality if it is fit for its intended use (by customers) in operations, analytics, decision-making, and planning. To be fit for use, data must be "free from defects" (i.e., "right") and "possess desired features" (i.e., be the "right data").*[18]

It drives home the importance of customers and recognizes that data quality is a multi-dimensional beast, requiring both that the data be correct and clearly defined, and that it be relevant to the task at hand.

My aspirational definition aligns with the longer-term goal of building a future in data:[19]

---

[17] This definition stems from my understanding of Dr. Joseph Juran's definition of quality, focused on the quality of manufactured product.

[18] I've used most of this definition for some time. Now, with the rise of big data and advanced analytics, I'm adding "analytics" to the mix and explicitly recognizing data scientists and other analysts as customers.

[19] I first used this definition in *Data Driven*.

*Exactly the right data in exactly the right place and right time and in the right format to complete an operation, serve a customer, conduct an analysis, craft a plan, make a decision, or set and execute strategy.*

This definition is especially helpful when imagining the organization unshackled from the constraints imposed by current realities.

To be a good customer, you have to build communication channels. Figure 3.1 represents this graphically. It depicts the customer-supplier model, modified slightly to emphasize these rights and responsibilities. As usually presented, one generally puts oneself (or one's process, department, function, etc.) in the middle, with suppliers on the left and customers on the right. I've split the "your process" symbol in half, with the right half emphasizing your role as data customer and the left as data creator for the next person in line. The main left-to-right arrows represent the flow of data, inputs and outputs, respectively.

Figure 3.1 The customer-supplier model with minor modifications to reflect your responsibilities as a data customer, to build and maintain high-bandwidth communications (requirements and feedback) channels with your most important data suppliers.

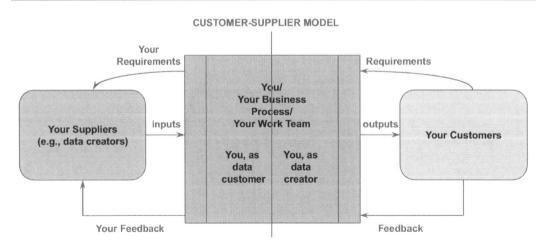

Of special importance here are the communication channels, specifically your requirements and your feedback to your most important data suppliers. If these

In the next chapter, on your roles as data creator, I'll urge you to take similar responsibilities for the communications channels with your customers.

channels don't exist, you must build them, make sure they operate effectively, expand them as necessary (I'll call this "broadband communications"), and maintain them–forever.

## COMMUNICATE YOUR NEEDS

Figure 3.2 presents a simple process that I've found enormously effective for developing a deeper understanding of your needs and requirements as a data customer, documenting them as the *voice of the customer* (*VoC*) and communicating them to suppliers.

I'm sure there are plenty of good methods to clarify your data needs. So if you have a method you use regularly, no need to learn this one. But if not, don't hunt around. This process is almost guaranteed to yield a good result the first time you use it and excellent results as you gain more experience.

Figure 3.2 Customer Needs Analysis Process (customer version).

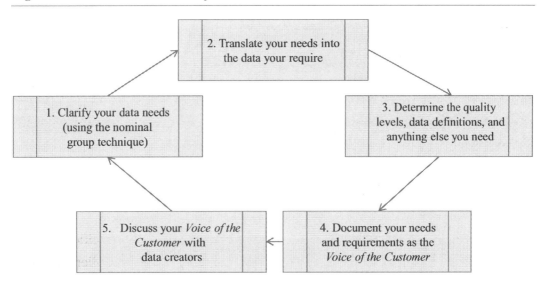

I'll explain a couple of key instructions for using this process below. But first I wish to make clear that a list of counterexamples does not constitute a usable *VoC*. You have to explain, in sufficient detail, what quality data looks like, in the customer's eyes.[20]

### Distinguish needs from solutions, features, or requirements

I find it helpful in the short term, and most beneficial in the long term, for customers to distinguish their needs from their requirements. The distinction may seem maddeningly subtle, so let me illustrate with an example. Those who drive family cars don't have the in-depth technical knowledge to articulate specifications such as:

> It is almost always better to tell your data suppliers what you need, in contrast to telling them how to give you what you need. If they know what you want, many of them will think creatively about new ways to satisfy your needs.

> *"We need the glass to be polarized, 0.17" thick, tempered for 40 hours in an 800 degree Thermaflex kiln, with a 26 percent blue-green tint, cut within 14 mils of specification, and with the edges sanded with 500 grit paper."*

Rather, they talk about what they need the glass to do, saying:

> *"We need to be able to see out in all kinds of weather. We want to be kept safe. We don't want to be blinded by the sun. We need the door to sound solid when it closes."*

The second quote articulates needs; the first, the requirements of the windshield-production process. It's the manufacturer's job to sort out the requirements for producing and installing a windshield that meet your needs.

Thus, step 1 calls for you to clarify your data needs. Statements beginning with "I need *to*" – as opposed to "I need *a*" – do this well. Examples of needs are:

---

[20] You can include some counterexamples in your *VoC* document, perhaps as an Appendix.

- "I need to track sales progress against plans on a weekly basis."
- "I need to set up corporate bonds the day before they go to market so we can sell them. I need all of the details that can impact pricing for a bond at that time."
- "I need to prepare the corporate report by the fifth business day after the end of each quarter, which means I'll need to have each unit's complete financials by day three."

State your needs in your own words, providing as much color and detail as you can. After all, data creators are far more likely to do careful work when they understand the purpose than when they're just filling out a form.

### Translate your needs into the data and anything else you require

The next two steps go further. For example, "I need to track sales progress against plan" may mean that you need:

1. The yearly plan, or target, for the number of units sold, for each SKU; or
2. The actual number of units manufactured, assigned to distributors, and sold at the retail level for each SKU, every week.

Further, you may require that:

a. A week starts at 12:01AM EST Monday and ends at midnight on Sunday. Note that the requirement defines a "week." You need the numbers by 8:00AM on the first Wednesday after each week.
b. Numbers provided must be within 3 percent of the actual units sold. If a number is missing, there should be a good explanation.
c. You need a contact to discuss anything that you don't understand.

This may seem like a lot of work (and it can be). It underscores why you should focus first on your most important needs.

## Document, document, document

The older I get, the more insistent I become that your *VoC* be written (not oral). Figure 3.3 provides an outline. The document need not be long – I've seen some great *VoCs* that were only seven pages or so.

Figure 3.3 Generic outline for a *Voice of the Customer* document.

1. Introduction and summary
2. Customers and their uses of data by:
   - Key decision makers
   - Process owners
   - Regulators
   - Etc.
3. Data required to meet these needs
   - Records and fields
   - Data dictionaries
   - Business rules
4. Data quality requirements
   - For data values (e.g., accuracy)
   - For data dictionaries (e.g., required data definition)
   - For data access (e.g., how data is delivered)
   - Other (e.g., timing)
5. Gap analysis (optional)
6. Version control

## Sit down with data suppliers

The data you need might be created by many different groups and accessed through intermediaries. For example, you may access financial data created in the Widget department via a data warehouse (see Figure 3.4). You can't expect the data warehouse group to do much about your accuracy requirements; nor can you expect the Widget department to do much about your access requirements. So the practical reality is that you'll have to sit down with each (perhaps together, but probably not). You should discuss the entire *VoC* document and decompose the requirements into those that the data warehouse group and the Widget department can handle, respectively.

Figure 3.4 Having multiple data suppliers compels you to decompose your overall requirements.

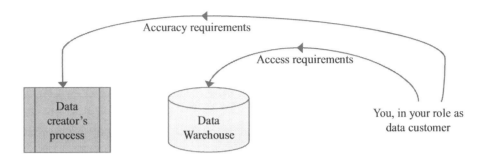

As another example, you may well need the end-of-day price for a given equity. That data is created on an exchange and you obtain it via a contracted market-data provider. In this case you should generally expect the market-data provider to work with the data creator on your behalf.

> To communicate with your data creators, you have to know who they are. That can be a challenge. You may simply look at a report, draw data from a data warehouse, or otherwise be unaware of its origin. A little detective work, starting from your source (or supplier) and working backward, should help you find the relevant data creators.

Note that neither the market-data provider nor the data warehouse is a data creator, even though they are your source or supplier. So I'll use the term "data supplier" to mean the person or group through which you obtain the data you need. A data supplier can be a data creator, but not always.

It is not enough to send your *VoC* document to data creators and suppliers electronically. You must sort out who the right people are and meet them face-to-face. You must explain why you are reaching out, why they are so important to you, how you use the data that they create or supply on your behalf. You need to give them time to ask questions and think. And while you should be flexible in terms of how you work together, you should pointedly ask them to work with you. In particular, you should ask them to:

1. Measure the quality of data they provide.
2. Identify and eliminate root causes of error.
3. Help shut down hidden data factories.

*To gain traction,* you don't need to engage all of your data suppliers; one will do just fine. Mark yourself as having gained traction when that supplier accepts your requirements and completes one improvement project. And mark yourself as having *achieved your first real result* when that supplier has completed three or four – you should notice a real difference at that time. And you'll have some real experience.

As you move to *the next level,* you should formalize this new way of working with data creators.

### What if you can't find data you know exists?

This situation comes up far too often, frustrating people and leading to all sorts of odd behavior. It usually arises because there are no requirements that data creators store what they create in an accessible manner or they maintain weak processes to ensure that they do so. It is another example of what happens when data customers are too tolerant. So if you and your team are spending too much time looking for and not always finding data you know is out there somewhere, follow the instructions given in this chapter: Spell out your needs, communicate them to the right supplier, and grow intolerant if you don't see rapid progress.

## INNOVATE AND ENCOURAGE INNOVATION

A healthy organization asks itself new questions all of the time and it will need new data to answer them. And sometimes your needs are quite vague. Suppose you're a senior executive, contemplating how you should acquire another company. Or you want data that will help you brainstorm new product ideas.

Use such new needs to spur innovation, both on your part and on the part of data creators. Follow the steps described here, emphasizing why you need what you need, providing as much context as you can. Give data creators the opportunity to meet your needs in ways that you couldn't have imagined.

Using the acquisition example, you might say, "I need to figure out a fair price for acquiring the XYZ Company. They have a reputation for customer allegiance, which may play a real role in the valuation. I need to know more, but I'm not sure what to ask." That's a perfectly respectable request for data, and there are many ways to approach it. So don't overspecify!

In almost all new situations, I find it best to simultaneously:

- Cast a wide net by acquiring disparate data that may be loosely defined, or of suspect quality. I'm even interested in data that may not bear directly on the topic at hand.
- Seek a smaller amount of carefully defined and created data that I feel certain I understand and can trust, even if it has other limitations.

It's likely to get you what you need. At first, the new data will almost certainly have deficiencies—it may involve only a small sample, the data definitions may prove imprecise, or some measurements may look suspect. This is natural, so use this data fully aware of its shortcomings. And demand rapid improvements!

> This don't over specify instruction is also important when it comes to bad news, including poor results, new threats, previously unforeseen risks, and so forth. Make clear the sort of things you want to be kept informed about, while also making it clear that, since these things are new, unexpected, or unforeseen, you can't possibly specify them in advance.

## ACTIVELY MANAGE BOTH INTERNAL AND EXTERNAL SUPPLIERS

As you gain experience in your role as a data customer, it is often appropriate to manage your data creators in a more formal, repeatable manner. Indeed, any external company with whom you contract for data should be actively managed.

Similarly, almost all important internal data creators should be managed formally.

> I find that almost all data creators respond well when engaged as called for here. The secret lies in thinking through what's in it for them (not just you) and approaching them with that in mind. A few may be defensive, believing their quality is high. If so, don't hesitate to show them a FAM, adding, "Here's our view of how you're doing."

A corporate finance group, in particular, should manage all departments on whose data it depends in this way. If the data is important and coming from somewhere other than your team, you should probably actively manage the data creator (or supplier). Figure 3.5 presents my preferred means of doing so.

Figure 3.5 Data Creator (Supplier) Management Cycle.

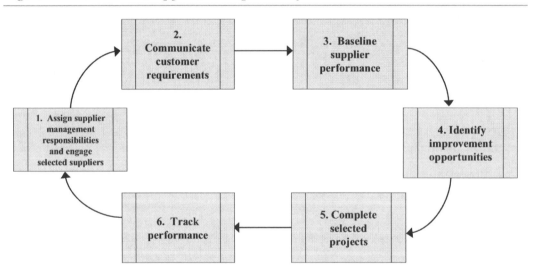

So far, I've discussed step 2, communicating your requirements. A couple of further remarks here: The first step is to name a person or team to work with each specific supplier (an embedded data manager is a good choice to lead a part-time team) and clarify his, her, or the team's responsibilities to improve supplier quality. "Halve the error rate in six months" is a good starting point. Don't skip this step – clarity in expectations is critical. And don't be afraid to try something new, gain some experience, and modify expectations.

Having done that, the obvious next step is to measure quality against those needs, then work with the data creator to identify and complete projects to close the gaps. You can, of course, measure performance and identify improvement projects on your own, but you can't actually conduct those projects; the data creator must do that. So in most circumstances, I find it best that data creators take the lead role or, alternatively, that you complete the remaining steps in the cycle together.

## MAKE YOUR HIDDEN DATA FACTORIES EXPLICIT AND EFFICIENT

While your long-term goal is to make hidden data factories as small as possible, in the near term it is wise to make them effective. After all, you have to protect yourself.

**Data factories represent non-value-added work**

A needed first step may involve shining a light on hidden data factories. Figure 3.6 presents two versions of a simple two-step process. In the first version, both steps work well. In the other, department B must implement a hidden factory to accommodate errors created by department A, most of which are corrected, though some leak through to customers.

As your data needs grow and change, on occasion you'll almost certainly need to experiment with new data from new suppliers of unknown quality. Initially, it may be impossible or not worth the effort to clarify your needs to these new data creators. After all, much of their data may turn out to be useless. In these circumstances, a hidden data factory can help you ensure that the new data is usable enough. That's why it isn't always possible, or even wise, to completely eliminate data factories.

The key observation is this: No fully-informed external customer would pay you more for the second version compared to the first. Said differently, *the hidden data factory creates no value in the customer's eyes – it is non-value-added work.*

Figure 3.6 Two versions of a two-step process. No customer would pay extra for steps to correct data and make good on errors that leak through. Thus, they represent non-value-added work.

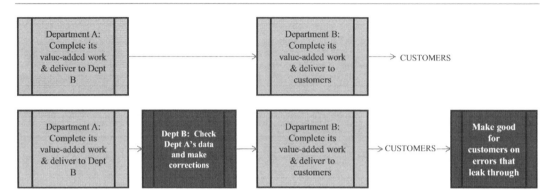

Now in the very near term, you probably have to continue to do this work. As I've noted, it is simply irresponsible to use bad data or pass it onto a customer. At the same time, all good managers know that, over time, they must reduce such work.

## Implement better controls

Most hidden data factories don't work all that well. Consider Samantha from earlier. Her assistant's control method is to give the Widget department's data a once-over and make any corrections that seem warranted. It's better than nothing, but the assistant knows little about widgets – it was just dumb luck that he was able to make a correction. Perhaps worst of all, his informal system may provide a false sense of security that the data is correct.

Chances are your data quality controls are equally informal and riddled with shortcomings. Four types of controls, as listed in Table 3.1, can help you make your data factories more effective. Use the table to develop increasingly better controls.

Here are four ways to do just that:

1. Implement *customer-found error control*. Samantha's assistant Steve should revert every issue he finds back to the Widget department and ask it to make the correction, rather than fixing the data himself.

2.  Institute *on-receipt control*. Rather than looking at the data when Samantha needs it, her assistant could look at the data when it is received. This would give him more time to make a correction, should the data be flawed.

3.  Get the Widget department to assume responsibility for the control before it sends the data out (data suppliers can perform most controls just as easily as you).

4.  Automate the controls: Many controls, especially portions that identify errant data, should be automated (making corrections often requires human intervention).

Table 3.1 Commonly employed customer data quality controls.

| Type of control | What it is | Comments |
|---|---|---|
| **On-receipt validation controls** | Employing proofreading or business rules. Identify and correct "invalid" data upon receipt from a data supplier. | Unless the data supplier is providing them, usually a good idea. |
| **On-use validation controls** | Employing proofreading or business rules. Identify and correct "invalid" data as a first step in using them. | Unless the data supplier is providing them, usually a good idea. |
| **Clean-up controls** | Usually employing business rules, identify and correct large quantities of invalid data, hopefully before they are used. | As a matter of best practice, should only be employed once the process of data creation works well (ensuring one-time only clean-up). There are exceptions based on business necessity. A "second-time clean-up" is indicative of an unhealthy data quality program. |
| **Customer-Found Error Control** | Correct errors that customers find. | Always. If customers are good enough to advise you of your errors, you should act quickly. |

## Build Organizational Capability

It is difficult and time consuming to sort out what you need, translate your needs into requirements, and work with data creators and suppliers to make sure they understand. You must assign people to the effort, as called for in Figure 3.7 and Table 3.2.

Figure 3.7 Build organizational capabilities to become a good data customer.

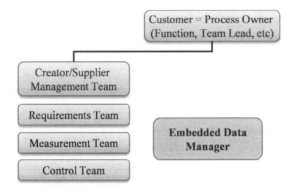

Table 3.2 Who does what for a good data customer.

| Who | Responsibility |
|---|---|
| Head of data customer's organization | Sets a tone and a change of direction in dealing with data suppliers. |
| Supplier Team | Oversees the data supplier management cycle. |
| Requirements Team | Develops and communicates the *Voice of the Customer.* |
| Measurement Team | Interprets measurements provided by data suppliers, helps others interpret them, and helps identify improvement projects (note: there is no formal improvement team). |
| Control Team | Brings the hidden data factory into the light, works to make the overall system of controls (including those conducted by the data supplier) more effective, and, as the data improves, works to shrink the hidden data factory. Responsible for the overall system of controls. |
| Embedded Data Manager | Assists with all of the work, leadership on some. |

## IN SUMMARY

If you need high-quality data to do your job, then you have to become a good customer, and as this chapter makes clear, doing so involves some hard work. You need to sort out what you need, translate your needs into requirements, and work with data creators and suppliers to make sure they understand. But there are no shortcuts!

Bear in mind that none of this is nearly as hard, or as time-consuming, as running a hidden data factory. The resulting improvements, to both the data and your network of data creators that know you and understand your needs, more than justify the effort.

Table 3.3 Data customer's indicators of success.

| You've | When |
|---|---|
| Gained Traction | You successfully communicated your *Voice of the Customer* to one data supplier and that supplier has made one real improvement. |
| Achieved Real Results | That supplier has completed several improvement projects such that you can see it in the data they send and can shrink a hidden data factory as a result. |
| Make it to the Next Level | You're actively managing both internal and external suppliers of all of the most important data. |

# CHAPTER 4, Part I
## Must-Dos for All Data Creators

In Chapter 3, I presented two definitions of data quality, each emphasizing the moment of use. My third definition emphasizes the moment of creation:

*Meeting the most important needs of the most important customers.*[21]

I call this my day-in, day-out definition, and it serves as a beacon for all data creators.

Data creators include people—after all people enter data and, in so doing, fit any reasonable definition of data creator. That goes for decision makers and planners as well. Their decisions and plans can be likened to data that guide the organization going forward. Data scientists, who tease out insights from large quantities of data, certainly count as data creators.

A measurement device, such as a weather station, a thermometer, a Fitbit, or any other connected tool, also qualifies. A computer application that copies a data item does not qualify. But one that takes $US PROFIT converts it to €US PROFIT and adds it to €EUROZONE PROFIT to produce €TOTAL PROFIT surely qualifies. Since a data customer cannot discuss his or her requirements with a device or bit of code, I find it more appropriate to view the person responsible for such as a data creator also.

Finally, I find it powerful to embed the act of data creation within a process and jointly consider both the process and its manager to be a data creator.

---

[21] The late Dr. William Barnard, of The Juran Institute, taught me this definition.

There are four must-do tasks for data creators: understanding customers and their needs, measuring against those needs, conducting improvement projects to close gaps, and implementing controls to keep errors from coming back. Data creators must do these things well and they are the subjects of the first part of this chapter.

The process management cycle helps data creators complete these must-dos and provides many other advantages. It is also my preferred means to unite the roles of data creator and data customer. But not all companies adopt process management in a formal way. Still, anyone can, and in my view should, use the process management cycle to full advantage. I consider these topics so important that I've reserved the second part of this chapter to cover it.

A section at the end of Chapter 4, Part II provides special instructions for the creation of data definitions.

**Instructions:**

1.  Recognize that you are a data creator and that the data you create impacts others.
2.  Focus on the most important needs of your most important customers. Spread the *Voice of the Customer* far and wide. Quit doing things that customers don't care about.
3.  Measure data quality levels as close to the points of data creation as possible.
4.  Complete improvement projects, identifying and eliminating root causes of error, to close the gaps between customer needs and measured quality levels.
5.  Implement a multi-layer program of control, in part to reduce the costs associated with the hidden data factory.
6.  Look for opportunities to innovate.

## RECOGNIZE YOU ARE A DATA CREATOR AND THAT YOUR WORK IMPACTS OTHERS

Just as everyone must recognize their roles as data customers, they must also recognize their roles as data creators, with responsibilities to those who use that data. It is a

> It bears mention that data creators are also data customers and must work with their data suppliers to ensure they have the high-quality inputs they need to meet their customers' expectations.

powerful insight. Also one that, after a moment's reflection, is quite obvious.

So who counts as a data customer? Certainly all of the following:

- Bosses, including anyone in your management chain.
- You are a customer for some of the data you create.
- Internal customers, others within the company but not in your management chain, who use the data you create or supply.
- External company customers, who have a business relationship with your company, but don't explicitly pay for the data they receive. A bank's customers don't explicitly pay for statements, for example.
- Paying customers, who pay for the data in question. These customers are especially important to commercial data providers such as Morningstar and TeleTech.
- Shareholders.
- Regulators.
- Others who may use the data you provide, even though there is no formal business relationship. People who use government statistics and other data are customers of the department creating them, for example.

I suppose one could cite computers or application programs as customers, especially since some data feeds directly into them. But, so far, anyway, you can't talk to a computer about what's most important. View the person or work team responsible for the application as the customer instead.

You need to recognize that your work impacts customers, even if they are outside your reporting structure. Bad data may cause them extra work, result in a bad decision, or cost your company a customer. You don't work in isolation. Respect these people and their needs.

## FOCUS ON THE MOST IMPORTANT NEEDS OF THE MOST IMPORTANT CUSTOMERS

In the previous chapter, I described how a customer should document his, her, or its needs and communicate them to data creators. From the creator's perspective, the essence of that advice is exactly the same, but with the added discomfort of sorting out which customers are most important. Figure 4.1 captures this in a "step 0," added to the customer needs analysis process.

Figure 4.1 The customer needs analysis process (creator version).

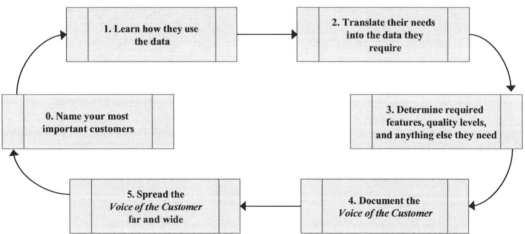

"Naming your most important customers" can be especially difficult because telling someone that another customer is more important can be uncomfortable. What should one do, for example, when the boss wants one thing and someone in a different department wants something else, even if the boss recognizes that department as a customer? There is no easy answer.

With some rather obvious modifications, steps 1 through 4 of the customer needs process unfold much the same whether the data customer or creator is leading the exercise. The result is a *Voice of the Customer* document. The last part of this instruction is spread the *VoC* far and wide. In contrast, the instruction for customers calls for a more targeted communication to critical data suppliers. Getting everyone involved can lead to immediate improvements, as when somebody notices, "Ah, I see why that is important. Until now I had simply put in 999-NA because someone taught me years ago that the system allowed it. Now that I know this is important, I can do much better."

As noted earlier, data creators failing to understand customer needs have been the major, if not dominant contributor to every data quality issue I've worked on for nearly 30 years. Fortunately, it is the easiest issue to resolve—no great technological magic is required. Unfortunately, I find many data creators reluctant to take this step—they feel it is tantamount to publicly admitting you don't know what the customer wants (in private conversations, many readily admit they don't understand customers or their needs. Their issue is admitting it publicly). My advice is simple, "Get over it!"

### Quit doing work for which you have no customer

I've used the term "non-value-added work" in connection with the hidden data factory, as work that no informed customer would pay extra for. You may still have to do this work. For example, you must correct an erroneous address for a customer before sending it out. Here I'm using the term "unimportant work," and it certainly qualifies as non-value-added. But it is distinct in that you don't have to do it.

Most people and work teams perform lots of unimportant work. For example, a market research group I worked with developed and sent out over 160 reports every week. This production effort occupied most of their time, leaving them little time to actually research the markets. So they rank-ordered these reports as best they could, based on whom they were sent to and the last time they fielded a question about them.

Next, they quit sending half, expecting a firestorm of complaints. But nary a peep! Ever.

So after a few weeks, they did it again, taking a bit more care rank-ordering the remaining 80 or so reports and again not sending out half. This time, they heard from one customer about one missing report. So they reinstated it. And they stopped the exercise. But note that they had eliminated three-quarters of their production work, freeing up valuable time for actual market research.

I find this again and again. People and work teams expend enormous effort on tasks for which they have no customer. So to be clear, understanding the needs of your most important customers does dual duty. It enables you to focus on what's most important and to ruthlessly cut work that is truly unimportant. It is NOT an instruction to cut staff. Rather, an instruction to redeploy staff to the most important work.

## MEASURE QUALITY AGAINST THOSE NEEDS, IN THE EYES OF THE CUSTOMERS

The next step is to measure the quality of data you, your work team, department or process creates against customer needs. Measurement is simultaneously the most mysterious and technical work in data quality management. Mysterious because data has no physical properties, such as length, viscosity, and color, so there is no physical property to record. Said differently, there is no such thing as an "accurometer."[22] Technical because there are often tough sampling issues to be resolved, complex measurement protocols to work out, and hard choices to be made about ways to report results. I've already discussed the Friday Afternoon Measurement as a means to gain traction. The next section looks at the "business

---

[22] I believe Bob Pautke made this observation.

rules" method, a popular means of scaling up. In the subsequent section I'll explore data quality measurements more generally.

## Scale up with business rules

The Friday Afternoon Measurement is fit for purpose in that it is fast, cheap, and provides a simple answer to a basic and important question. It is often perfect for getting traction. It does not, however, scale up. Over time, data creators must measure every month, week, day, or an even briefer period of time, depending on the speed of the process. Automated measurements are needed. That's where DQ Measurement with Business Rules comes in.

In this context, a business rule is nothing more than a constraint on data values. If the data values lie outside the specified domain, they can't be correct. Some examples of failed business rules and the reason they fail (in this particular case) include:

SUPPLIER NAME = NULL (a required attribute)

SEX = X (Sex = M, F, or NA only permitted)

REVENUE = $10,000; EXPENSE = $8,000; PROFIT = $4,000 (Profit must equal Revenue – Expense)

Thus the basic idea is to automate the checking of a data set against the rules, smacking data created in the most recent time period against the rules, and counting the failed records. Figure 4.2 presents the protocol.

Figure 4.2 Protocol for measuring data accuracy using business rules.

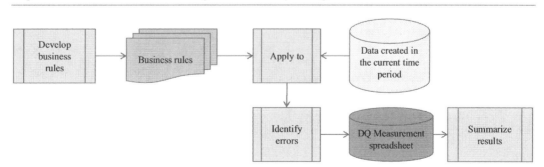

The power of automation allows frequent measurement. Hence the time-series plot, such as in Figure 4.3. It and the Pareto chart (Figure 4.4) are the workhorses of quality management.

Figure 4.3 Time-series plot example.

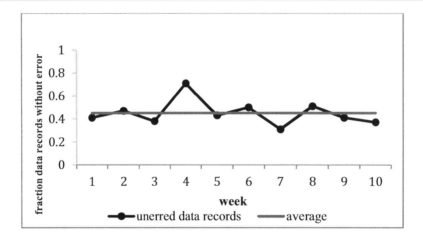

Figure 4.4 Pareto chart example.

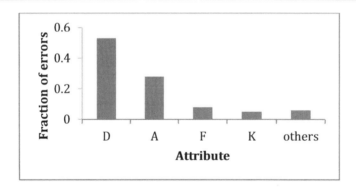

## A Broader Look at Data Quality Measurement

Commercial data providers should, in my opinion, publish data quality statistics, using time-series and Pareto plots.

The measurement methods introduced so far (Friday Afternoon Measurement, business rules measurements, and the rule-of-ten) are useful, even powerful. But they are not perfect, nor do they cover all situations that come up. Indeed, there are enough situations and measurement options to fill an entire volume. So I wish to conclude this section by providing two further instructions.

The first follows up on the earlier observation that there is no "accurometer." Thus, all methods for measuring data accuracy have strengths and weaknesses. The Friday Afternoon Measurement suffers because experts make mistakes and because it doesn't scale up. Measurements using business rules suffer because meeting a business rule doesn't imply that the data is correct. For example, for me, SEX = F is incorrect. But it will pass a simple business rule that SEX must be either M or F. Table 4.1 presents a list of measurement devices, a brief summary of how they work, and the pros and cons of each.[23]

Table 4.1 Candidate data accuracy measurement devices.

| Device | Description | Strength | Weakness |
|--------|-------------|----------|----------|
| **Data Tracking** | Track a sample of data records across an end-to-end process of data creation | powerful insights, focus on interfaces between steps | expensive |
| **Expert Opinion (i.e., Friday Afternoon Measurement)** | Experts identify errors by eye | quick and easy | doesn't scale |
| **Business Rules** | Compare data to business rules to identify "invalid" data | scale, linkage to control | more difficult than it seems |
| **Customer Complaint** | Counts errors customers complain about | measurement in the eyes of the customer | customers don't always (or even often) complain; deceptively hard |
| **Real-World** | Compare data to real-world counterparts | best accurometer | very expensive and not always feasible |
| **Surveys** | Ask customers | can yield powerful insights | often difficult to set up, administer, and interpret |

---

[23] See my paper on measuring data accuracy for a more complete discussion on crafting data accuracy measurements: "Measuring Data Accuracy: A Framework and Review," Contributed chapter in *Information Quality,* Advances in Management Information Systems Series, Armonk: M.E.Sharpe, 2005, pp. 21-36.

Use this list to develop more appropriate accuracy measurements as your data quality program matures.

Second, so far I've concentrated only on accuracy in the process of data creation. Yet other aspects of data quality may also be important.

## FIND AND ELIMINATE ROOT CAUSES OF ERROR

Eliminating root causes of error is essential if you're going to create data correctly the first time. Sometimes this is easy: Those who create data may, once they understand customer needs or quality levels (e.g., along the lines of Figures 4.3 and 4.4), act on their own accord to find and eliminate the root causes of error. You should encourage this!

In keeping with the emphasis on "who," I prefer QIC to Six Sigma because it clarifies the who right up front in step 1. That said, the last thing most organizations need is "dueling improvement methods." So if your company is comfortable with Six Sigma, by all means use it for data quality.

Sometimes eliminating the root cause is more involved and then it is best to employ a structured method. If yours is a Six Sigma company (meaning it regularly employs DMAIC, lean, lean-sigma, or a variant) then use it. If not, follow the Quality Improvement Cycle (QIC),[24] depicted in Figure 4.5. QIC was developed at AT&T in the 1980s and has proven itself time and again.

Except for the first two steps, which involve getting the right people in place, I'm not going to discuss QIC any further.

Step 1 of the QIC calls for the appropriate manager (work team, departmental, or process manager) to select improvement projects. He or she can identify potential

---

[24] *AT&T Quality Improvement Cycle*, AT&T, 1988.

projects using customer needs, measurements, perceived gaps, broken interfaces (see next section), or the inputs of others, and base their selection on any number of factors from anticipated benefits (e.g., cost reduction) to progress towards targets to the entreaties of those who work on the process to his or her own preferences to perceived ease or difficulty to political expediency. The point is that the choice of project falls to the responsible manager because he or she bears ultimate responsibility for results.

Figure 4.5 The QIC is a powerful method for identifying and eliminating root causes of data errors.

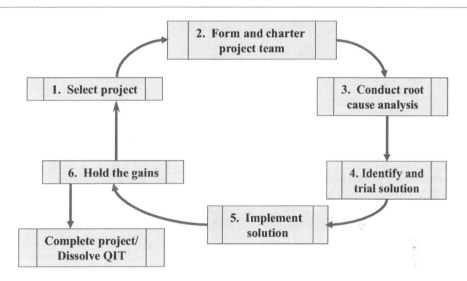

When getting started, I advise managers to select relatively simple projects, those that involve fewer data attributes, people, departments, and computer systems. Indeed, you need to complete at least one project to gain traction and several to claim real results. Further, there is a real sense of accomplishment, perhaps even euphoria, in completing an improvement project. Those participating are empowered, and achieve a dynamic that leads to continuous improvement. So, smart managers get those first few improvement projects under their belts.

Having selected the improvement project, the manager must then put the right improvement team in place and work with it to establish a charter. It's best to keep project teams as small as possible, but collectively, members of the team must have a full understanding of the steps where the issue occurs (i.e., the team must be able to surround the problem). This means that a more complex problem will require more people. One person should be designated team leader and another "facilitator."

My rule of thumb is that step two is complete only when the project team and process owner agree to a "charter," including a specific error reduction goal and time frame. Thus (from Figure 4.4), "reduce the error rate associated with attribute D by 50 percent in three months. Reduce it by a further 50 percent, for a total 75 percent reduction, in three more months" is an example of a good charter.

Once chartered, the improvement team works the remaining steps of the QIC and is disbanded when it completes its agreed project.

## ESTABLISH CONTROL

Dr. Juran defines control as "the managerial act of comparing actual performance against standards and acting on the difference."[25] It is a powerful synthesis that covers situations as diverse as managing your teenager's curfew to managing a complex organization. Figures 4.6 and 4.7 present the generic control flowchart and

> The term "governance" refers to the overall system of controls in a data (or any other) program.

flowchart for a common household thermostat respectively. Note that a hidden data factory is a form of control. An expensive and not-so-effective one, but it is a control nonetheless.

The long-term goals for an overall system of data quality controls include:

- Preventing errors at the point of data creation.

---

[25] I've always cited Joseph Juran, *Managerial Breakthrough*, McGraw-Hill, 1964 as the source of this quote. My apologies, but I can't find a page number. The definition is incredibly helpful, whether applied to quality or any other managerial activity.

- Detecting and correcting errors before they do any harm and ideally as quickly as possible.
- Responding to customer-found errors quickly.
- Ensuring that the overall quality program works as planned.
- For some processes, establishing statistical control, or stability.
- Error-proofing processes and measurement devices.
- Doing all of this in a cost-effective manner.

Figure 4.6 The generic control process after the work of Dr. Juran.

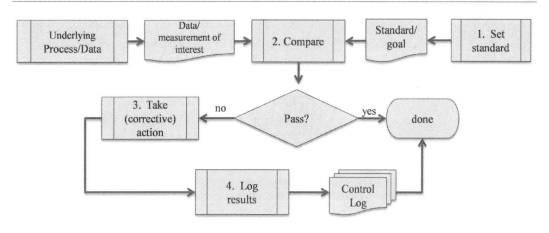

Figure 4.7 A thermostat effects control.

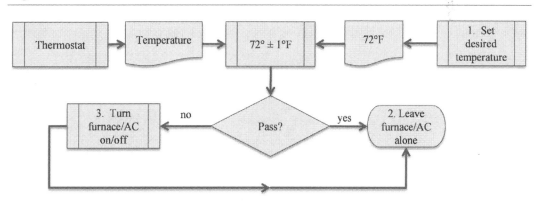

There are many types of data quality controls. See Table 4.2 for a list.

Table 4.2 Commonly used data creation controls.

| Type | Brief Description | When Appropriate |
|---|---|---|
| **Proofing** | Take a hard look at the data and make corrections as appropriate. | To gain traction, when business rules are poorly developed. |
| **Tail-end validation control** | Identify and correct "invalid" data using business rules at the end of the day. | To scale up for real results. For sophisticated rules involving multiple attributes. |
| **In-process validation control** | Identify and correct "invalid" data using business rules as the data is created. Note: Many good web-based forms don't let you move on until data you entered pass rules. | For many rules, these validation controls are superior to tail-end controls because they are more effective and cheaper. |
| **Customer-found error control** | Correct errors that customers find. | Always. If customers are kind enough to advise you of your errors, you should act quickly. |
| **In-factory calibration** | Ensure that measurement equipment measures correctly before the device leaves the factory. | To scale up for real results or getting to the next level. Always needed when there are many devices. |
| **In-use calibration** | Re-calibrate measurement equipment to ensure it measures correctly in real use. | To scale up for real results or getting to the next level. Always needed when there are many devices. |
| **Statistical process control** | Separate special causes from common causes to establish a basis for predicting future process performance. | For relatively fast-moving processes. |
| **Quality assurance = Audit controls.** | Ensure that the overall data quality program is working as designed. | As you get real results and getting to the next level. |

I find that many data creators initially employ no controls whatsoever. A simple control or two helps gain traction, then points the way to real results and the next level. So consider the process that produced the data in Figure 4.3. A simple control that called for "eyeballing data created yesterday and making needed corrections at 8:00AM today" would make for a big step up. It is obviously not a perfect control. But people, even non-experts, are quite good at spotting errors, and such a control will catch most of the obvious errors and some of the subtle ones. It is a big step up from no control whatsoever.

To solidify results and scale up, the next step is to use business rules (the same business rules used for measurement) to detect errors as the data is created.

> This control is akin to asking someone to proofread an important report before you send it on and perfectly appropriate for unstructured data.

If an attribute fails a rule, the control alerts the data creator to correct the value before loading the data.

Finally, statistical process controls help get to the next level.

To conclude this section, I'd like to contrast two controls, applied to the same data, one by the data customer and the other by the data creator. In the example, in step 1, a customer order is created (perhaps the customer is placing the order over the Internet or phoning it in) and in the second, three days later, his or her products are taken from the warehouse and shipped. Of special interest here is the customer's address and suppose the following is entered:

City, State, Zip Code, Country = Rumson, NJ, 90210, USA

The obvious error is that the (city, state) pair and the zip code don't align—one or both is incorrect.

Now the shipping clerk, who has to deal with returns, may eyeball the address and

> Luckily, more and more web-based forms employ such controls. Move controls as close to the moments of data creation as you can. Doing so not only makes for better controls, it enables data customers to reduce the size and complexity of their hidden data factories.

notice this error. But it will likely take considerable effort to find the correct address (as the rule of ten suggests).

A better control, built into the data entry application, would signal the inputter of the error and require correction before moving on. The cost of correction is far, far less!

## INNOVATE, INNOVATE, INNOVATE

Data creators should always be on the lookout for ways to innovate. Of particular interest here are:

- Adding a new feature (i.e., a new data attribute, way of viewing the data, etc.) to data you already deliver to customers. Frankly, you should approach this the same way you approach improvement—always have at least a project or two in the works.
- Developing wholly new data. Here is where a deep understanding of customer needs comes into play. For there are always unmet customer needs, for new data, deeper insights, a different look, and so forth—often needs that they cannot fully articulate. Focus especially on leading-edge customers, those who are thinking further out into the future. Work with them to articulate those unmet needs. Then figure out new ways to meet them.

## IN SUMMARY

You need high-quality data from others to do your job and it is only right that the data you create and pass on meet the needs of the next person or team. You must view them as customers and treat them as such. Frankly, in most cases this is not nearly as hard, nor as time consuming, as it might seem at first. You'll make your customers and your company stronger. And if you're first in your company to do so, you'll set a real standard for others.

Following the instructions here enables you to create results as depicted in Figure 4.8. Each milestone bears a letter corresponding to a phase in the overall program; T for gaining traction, RR for achieving real results, and NL for getting to the next level. Consider that "traction has been gained with the completion of the first improvement project and the first real result is achieved when the initial target is met. Notice in particular, the promised order of magnitude improvement. So get on with it!

Figure 4.8 "Milestones" in the advance of a data quality program.

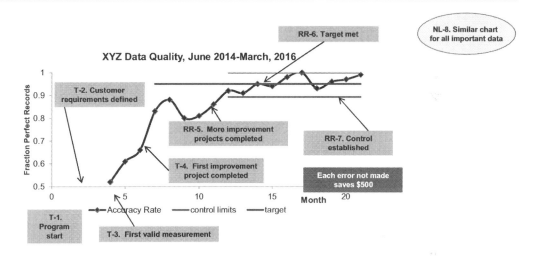

Table 4.3 Indicators of success

| You've | When |
|---|---|
| Gained Traction | You've successfully understood the needs of one important customer, made a measurement against those needs, and made one real improvement. |
| Achieved Real Results | You've completed several improvement projects such that you've made a real difference for at least one customer. |
| Make it to the Next Level | You're actively managing data creation such that all your most important customers are enjoying increasingly higher-quality data. |

A s used here, a "process is any sequence of work activities, characterized by common inputs and outputs and directed to a common goal."[26] Simple enough. But note that the term, in and of itself, applies equally well to the simple task of making yourself a cup of coffee as it does to multi-year efforts to integrate departments after a multi-billion dollar merger. Here we are primarily interested in the data-creating aspects of a process. Thus the process of "making yourself a cup of coffee" does produce a cup of coffee. It may also produce data, as in a note "buy more coffee."

I call simple processes "little-p processes." Taking customer orders and invoicing customers are good examples. Each produces a small amount of basic (and important) data. The term "little-p" is relative—little-p processes usually involve only a single team, a unit of work can be completed in a few hours or days, and the actual work is often conducted within a single department, with few organizational interfaces or handoffs.

Little-p processes are almost always parts of larger ones. For a hospital, the most important process may start when a patient checks in, moves to her room, goes through a sequence of clinics, operating theaters, and labs, and concludes when all of the bills are paid. The associated data creation and usage are also part and parcel of a "Big-P Process." Organizations, even massive ones, have no more than a dozen or so Big-P Processes. Middle-p processes occupy the ground in between.

---

[26] *Process Quality Management & Improvement Guidelines, Issue 1.1*, AT&T Quality Steering Committee, 1998.

**Instructions:**

1.  Manage data creation as a process.
2.  Vest overall responsibilities for high-quality data creation in a process owner or process management team.
3.  Extend the voice of the customer to align work in the direction of the customer.
4.  Look for opportunities to improve on the interfaces between steps. In doing so, complement functional management.
5.  Build organizational capabilities. Process managers must learn to lead through influence, not formal authority.
6.  Employ an "embedded data manager," with solid expertise in the "how-tos" of doing this work effectively.

One especially important process involves the creation of data definitions and all the instructions of both parts of this Chapter apply. Still, there is an underlying dynamic and some subtleties that those responsible for this work must understand if they are to be effective. The final section of this Chapter explores these and summarizes special instructions.

## MANAGE DATA CREATION AS A PROCESS

See Figure 4.9, which presents the process management cycle.[27] From a data perspective, process management "works" for four inter-related reasons. First, it aligns the work in the direction of the customer. Without process management, customers, other than the boss, receive short shrift.

Second, this alignment helps bridge silos between work teams and departments. This is a big deal—earlier I had noted that a poor connection between customers and data creators contributed to every data quality problem I have worked on.

---

[27] To the best of my knowledge the process management and improvement cycle was developed at AT&T Bell Laboratories in the late 1980s. I've made a modification of two, based primarily on my tastes.

That problem also arises during the creation of more complex data products, especially those that require contributions from several creators working in silos that "don't talk."

Figure 4.9 Process management cycle.

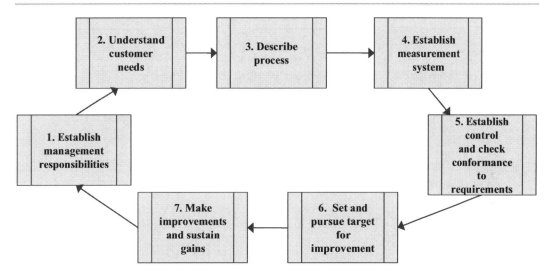

Third, the process framework clarifies managerial responsibilities for data creation, the "who" this book promises.

Fourth, the process framework is unmatched at bringing the tasks described in Part I into a powerful, coherent whole. You have to do them anyway. You should do them in a powerful way!

I've already discussed the basics for some steps. In the remainder of this chapter I'll expand on select topics.

## CLARIFY MANAGERIAL RESPONSIBILITIES

I can't overemphasize the importance of clear managerial responsibilities for data creation. The process management cycle takes care of that right up front, in step 1. The basic idea is that a "process manager" (be it a single executive/owner/manager or, if the process is large and complex, a process management team) is held accountable for end-to-end performance. From a data perspective, this means delivering high-quality data to customers at a reasonable cost. In some cases, data creation is the raison d'être; in other cases, physical product may also be created or moved.

A reasonable starting point for working out accountabilities includes:

- A mid-term quality target, such as "Within two years, have in place a quality program such that our most important customers receive far better data from us."
- Authorities to effect changes to meet the target (e.g. budget, staffing, process design).
- Authority to import or build the skills needed to complete the work called for throughout the process management cycle.

Process management stands in contrast to functional management in that it points horizontally, across tasks, functions, and departments, in the direction of the customer. Functional management points vertically, up and down the management chain. Many people fall into the trap of viewing the two as competing management styles, but I find that shortsighted. Functional management promotes the effective and efficient completion of tasks, and it is incredibly important that tasks be completed well. Process management, on the other hand, aims to knit tasks together into a more powerful whole.

Effective process managers take steps that help them add enormous value while avoiding the more obvious conflicts with functional management, as described in the following sections.

## EXTEND THE VOICE OF THE CUSTOMER

Effective process managers spend an enormous amount of time building communications channels, emphasizing the *Voice of the Customer*, and aligning the work in the direction of the customer. Importantly, they recognize that people's bosses are customers.

Figure 4.10 presents a more complex process, featuring three suppliers, four customers, and six steps. As the figure depicts, an effective process owner not only makes sure that all hear the voice of the customer, but that everyone understands the needs of the next step. This effort extends to data suppliers, both outside the process and the entire company.

Figure 4.10 Effective process managers seemingly go overboard in communications, fixing broken or non-existent requirements channels, and aligning work groups in the direction of the customer.

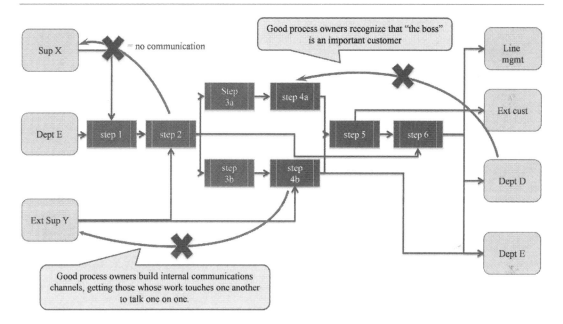

## LOOK FOR IMPROVEMENT OPPORTUNITIES ON THE INTERFACES BETWEEN TASKS/STEPS

I've mentioned several times that a contributing factor to every data quality issue I've worked on for nearly 30 years has been the failure of data creators to understand customer

> I sometimes say that "silos are the enemy of data quality" because they make much of the basic communications that data quality requires more difficult.

needs. A second factor is broken interfaces between steps needed to deliver on those needs. Work team and departmental silos often lie at the root of the issue. Each team bears responsibility for its own work, but neither feels responsible for the interface. But process owners, with their end-to-end view, do have such responsibilities.

Consider Figure 4.11. Here the focus is shortening the end-to-end cycle time associated with the process, currently seven days. Note that the actual work takes one day, while the remaining six days are spent in queues. Cutting the actual work time in half would take considerable effort and only shorten the total time to 6.5 days. So the effective process owner focuses instead on the queue time, the time between steps, on the interfaces between work teams, when no real work is accomplished. It's far easier to shorten queue time by improving these interfaces. Here, cutting queue time in half saves three days. Further, it is far easier to get those responsible for steps to work together on such efforts.

Figure 4.11 To shorten cycle time, process owners focus first on "queue time" between steps, not on the way the steps are performed.

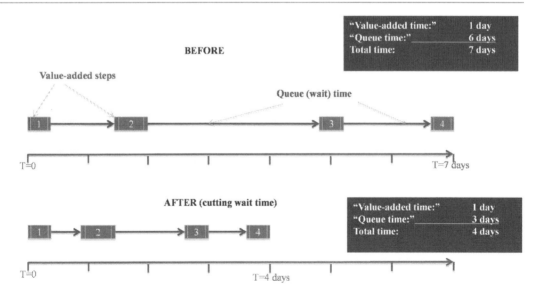

## BUILD ORGANIZATIONAL CAPABILITIES

Figure 4.12 proposes the "getting started" organizational structure for data creators in the context of the process management cycle (modify it as needed if you don't use process management). Key features include a process owner (or depending on the size of the process, a process management team). Other teams complete the work associated with data creation, on behalf of the process's data customers. The embedded data manager assists.

Figure 4.12 Recommended organizational structure for data creation.

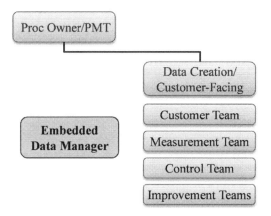

Note that the figure explicitly assigns sub-teams to complete steps 2, 4, 5, and 7, respectively, of the process management cycle. The complete list of who does what follows in Table 4.4.

Table 4.4 Who does what in data creation.

| no. | Step | Who | Rationale |
| --- | --- | --- | --- |
| 1 | Managerial Responsibilities | Process Owner/PMT | PMT must negotiate responsibility and authority. |
| 2 | Understand customer needs | Customer Team | Helps if this work is performed in an ongoing fashion. Having a team that does this (it's part-time work) helps build skill and sort out commonalities among customers. |

| no. | Step | Who | Rationale |
|---|---|---|---|
| 3 | Understand current process | PMT | This work is usually performed one time (with incremental changes as the process changes). While the PMT may contract the work out, it does not justify a standing team. |
| 4 | Measure against customer needs | Measurement Team | Some specialized expertise needed. |
| 5 | Establish control | Control Team | Some specialized expertise needed. |
| 6 | Set targets | PMT | Akin to setting responsibilities, step 1. |
| 7 | Make improvements | PMT and Improvement Team | The PMT selects improvement projects and gets the right people on-board. From there the improvement team takes over. Note: Improvement teams are not standing teams. They disband when completing their work. |
|  | All. | Embedded Data Manager | Assistance with all steps, leadership on many. |

## Learn to manage cross-functionally

Managing a process, even one that crosses team lines within your department, can feel like herding cats. That feeling grows the larger the process gets, and the more work teams, departments, and people involved. After all, these things mean more cats. Worse, conflicts between vertically-oriented functional management and the horizontally-oriented process management are sure to arise. Effective process owners acknowledge these realities and work with them. Of course, the process management cycle is designed to help them do so effectively.

Still, being an effective process manager often requires more. Figure 4.13 presents a notion that I learned at AT&T's management charm school. The basic idea is simple: The inner circle represents one's "span of control," over things he or she can make happen, while the outer circle represents one's "span of influence," over things that one can impact, though not directly. As the figure depicts, process managers strive to increase their spans of influence. To be effective, process managers must accept that they have less control and learn how to build influence.

Figure 4.13 Process owners strive to increase their influence.

**Line/Functional Manager**

**Process Manager**

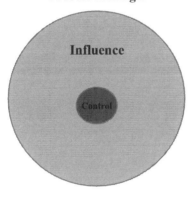

Traits of the effective process owner:
- The ability to lead through influence, rather than control,
- Nerves of steel and steely optimism,
- Strong written and verbal communications,
- Solid analytical and synthetic thinking,
- Able to make decisions and see them through,
- Able to negotiate across organizational boundaries,
- Able to build and coordinate a diverse team, and
- Perseverance, coupled with a strong sense of humor!

## EMPLOY EMBEDDED DATA MANAGERS

While the actual work involved in doing each of these steps is not technically difficult, it may be new and unfamiliar. Embedding expertise in the process moves the work along. I call the person with this expertise the embedded data manager. He or she takes lead responsibility for the measurement and control work and facilitates the customer needs and quality improvement teams. He or she also coordinates the process's contribution to company-wide initiatives, such as company-wide data quality targets and common definitions. As a practical matter, the embedded data manager knows the data, and helps

> It takes both training and experience to grow into the embedded data manager role. Plan on two to five days of formal training, encourage embedded managers to read extensively, and get them to join relevant professional associations. They'll grow more effective with experience as well. Expect about two years to become fully effective.

people interpret and use the data in new, creative ways. In many respects, the embedded data manager is "the tip of the spear" in a data quality program. It is an exciting, multi-faceted role.

A rule of thumb is that a solid data quality program requires about one embedded data manager per 100 people, more when the data or process is highly complex and many more for commercial relationships.

## The Fundamental Organization Unit for Data Quality

When I introduced the concepts of data customer and data creator in Chapter 1, I also pointed out that all of us play both data roles—sometimes simultaneously. We use data from others to do our work and others depend on our data to do theirs. While the two roles are separate, they are also linked.

This observation, coupled with my preference to view both roles in the context of process, leads me to Figure 4.14. I call it *the fundamental organization unit for data quality* owing to its power in describing the base capabilities companies must build.

Figure 4.14 Fundamental Organizational Unit for Data Quality unites the roles of data customers and data creators.

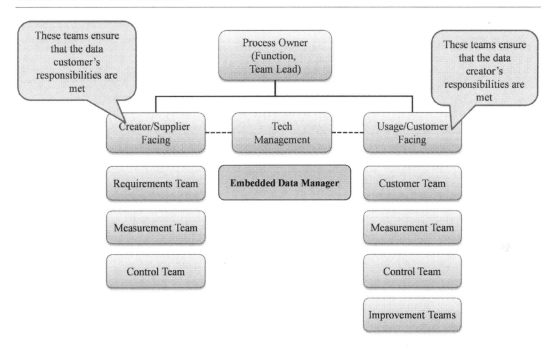

## SPECIAL INSTRUCTIONS FOR CREATING COMMON DATA DEFINITIONS

Few companies enjoy the benefits of clear, shared data definitions. While communications are just fine within silos, cross-departmental communications are strained, resulting in misunderstandings by data customers. Further, the computer systems that support those departments don't talk well, and translation requires massive hidden data factories. As noted earlier, the instructions of this Chapter apply, though to be effective, a deeper understanding of an underlying dynamic and some subtleties is needed.

### Underlying dynamic

I'll illustrate using two of my grandsons, here called Jack and Charlie. The action unfolds one morning, after the two of them had spent the night with me and my wife. They sleep in the same room at our house and they woke up at about 6:00

AM. But rather than screaming out for me and Grandma to come get them, they just talked to one another—for a good, long while. Finally one of them decided he was hungry and called out. And when my wife Nancy went into their bedroom, Jack said, "Charlie's hungry."

Now here's the interesting thing. Charlie, at 18 months, didn't know more than a few words of English. But it was clear enough that both he and his 4-year-old brother knew lots of words—enough to hold a 20-minute conversation. Those words were just in their own private vocabulary.

I find this vignette especially enlightening. A new language, let's call it the Jack–Charlie language, developed quickly in response to the specific needs of two brothers. It may die quickly as well. As Charlie learns new words in English a special language won't be critical.[28]

Of course this process is not confined to brothers. Specialized vocabularies develop to support new disciplines, new departments, new problems, and new opportunities. Words take on special, subtle, nuanced, and precise meanings, perfect for the circumstances and unsuitable for other settings. For example, in a team at AT&T I'll describe in Chapter 9, the terms "risk" and "consequence" took on quite specialized meanings. Unless you're stuck in a rut, this process is certainly occurring all over your company today, even as you read these words. Language constantly grows and divides.

> Many companies mistake metadata (descriptive information about the data) for an esoteric IT problem. After all, the issue often comes up when business language is translated into computer systems. But as this discussion clarifies, the issue is a business issue and must be addressed as such.

This process is normal and healthy, even essential to problem solving. You cannot, and should not, do anything to interfere. Quite the contrary, you

---

[28] I understand that twins often develop their own language much as Jack and Sawyer did, and build on it throughout their entire lifetimes.

should figure out how to take advantage.

In parallel, you must make sure there is enough common language so the company doesn't deteriorate into a Tower of Babel. Note that this is exactly what Jack did—using English to clue Nancy and me in on what they needed us to know.

Thus, to get in front of the language dynamic, follow these two simple rules:

**Rule 1:** Do all you can to encourage the growth of specialized language to meet specific needs, when and where needed. Insist on solid definitions for all terms, once they are used by more than a single work team.

**Rule 2:** Provide the skinniest common language as possible to facilitate company-wide communication.

In practice, this means creating a company-wide process for creating and documenting definitions of important business terms, communicating them through some sort of data dictionary, and building them into databases and applications. I'll use Aera Energy as an example in Chapter 9.

### Common language is not an IT issue

The Jack-Charlie vignette and the two rules apply to all companies and following them requires some skill. Before jumping into that, it bears mention that the need for common definitions usually comes up as the solution to an incompatible systems problem, as companies try to interconnect their systems. The accounting system doesn't talk to the sales system, which doesn't talk to the engineering system, and so on. The

> Of course, "systems not talking" is an overstatement. They do, eventually, as people work hard to translate the terms used in one system to the terms used in another. More on this in Chapter 8.

essence of the problem, though possibly not the details, is the same at all levels, from department to company to industry.

Since the "systems not talking" problem presents itself as a "systems problem," it is assigned to the IT department, which treats it as a data integration problem. And IT does the best it can. Assisted by a suite of tools, IT seeks to line up the systems, by translating the terminology (e.g., definitions of data item) used in one system to the terminology used in another. And vice versa. If there are n systems, that means roughly $n^2$ translations (though in practice there are fewer because not all systems need to talk to one another). Progress is almost always slow and fraught.

Sometimes IT tries to get in front and drive a common language across the enterprise. The effort goes by many names, such as data integration, enterprise architecture, and master data management. In doing so, it violates the spirit of rule 1 and the letter of rule 2, almost guaranteeing failure. It is akin to asking Jack and Charlie not to talk to each other since Charlie doesn't know enough English!

To say the same thing from a slightly different angle, the best computer systems faithfully represent the language employed by their users. Just as it is difficult for people to communicate when they don't share a common language, the same is true for computers. It is actually far worse for computers. Humans adapt and they adapt quickly. Computers, so far anyway, have proven considerably less adaptable. And they've not yet shown the ability to develop a new language, as Jack and Charlie did.

The fact that computers don't talk is not a computer problem. It is a language problem and it can only be solved as such.

**Manage the creation of data definitions as you would any other process:**

1.  Manage the creation of data definitions as an end-to-end process, with the goal of implementing the two rules noted above. Thus the process produces definitions for all key terms. A few should become common, shared definitions. I find it helpful to liken this portion of the process to forming international standards with a formal method for proposing

topics, soliciting the widest variety of standards, ample discussion, and a formal "vote."

2. That process must have an owner, perhaps called the Chief Data Architect. Since common definitions must reach across departments, this person should report to the leader of the Corporate Data Quality Team (Chapter 5), not to IT, emphasizing the point that data definitions are not the province of IT. This person must have the considerable personal gravitas needed to carry out this role.

3. Get the right people involved. Anyone whose work may be impacted by a common definition should have a say in its creation. Embedded data managers play an important role.

4. Publish all definitions via a data dictionary and make it easy for people to access that dictionary.

5. Socialize the common definitions more proactively.

6. Don't overreach. While hundreds of definitions are needed, even the most complex organization probably requires no more than 100 common ones. For example, Aera (Chapter 9) gets along just fine with 53.

7. Use all definitions, especially the common ones, in new systems development going forward.

## IN SUMMARY

Process management is the preferred framework for managing data creation. It is also a terrific framework for pulling the roles of creator and customer into a powerful whole. Even if your company doesn't do so, use it extensively. It is especially critical that you adopt a process framework in the creation of common data definitions.

# CHAPTER 5
# Provocateurs Disrupt Organizational Momentum

In Chapter 2, I explained the organizational momentum that causes people to set up hidden data factories. It is pretty basic. They encounter errors in the data they need to do their work and so they make corrections. It doesn't occur to them that they should reach back to the data creators. In time, dealing with errors just becomes a fact of business life. The dynamic occurs at the individual, work team, department, and company level. Left unchecked, hidden data factories pop up all over, virtually littering a company.

This is where provocateurs come in. They disrupt that momentum.

Lots of people see problems in their work but remain silent or simply whine about them. What distinguishes provocateurs is that they dig deeper and, when further steps are warranted, they take them.

## PROVOCATEURS LOOK TO IMPROVE THEIR CURRENT WORK

I've had the pleasure of working with provocateurs in industries as diverse as telecom, financial services, oil and gas, technology, and retail; a couple of government agencies; and at all levels of organizations, from individual contributors, to middle managers, to heads of business units. Each saw something they didn't like in their work environments and tried to make it better. I don't think any intended to be a provocateur. Certainly none had a "transformational vision" in mind when they started. Indeed, the problem or opportunity wasn't all that well-formed in their minds when they started. But it bothered them enough that they followed up.

Let's explore some examples. John Fleming, at Morgan Stanley, had inherited a group that absorbed "market data" such as corporate bond offerings, dividends, and mergers that would be pertinent to financial markets and loaded that data into corporate databases. His group worked with companies that sourced, organized, and licensed that data. They'd buy multiple copies of the same data, compare them, and load the data that looked best into the corporate store (this is the so-called "golden copy" approach). The data was used in many ways, from trading to servicing client accounts.

The reader will immediately see a hidden data factory here and an especially expensive one at that. At the very least, buying the same data from three sources immediately triples the cost. But that wasn't what troubled Fleming. What troubled him was that even the best "copy" wasn't all that great. There were enough complaints and he had enough experience to suspect the data was actually pretty bad.

Kim Russo led Marketing and Sales for a company that licensed tariff data needed by telecoms to bill their customers. These tariffs originate in the outputs of rate commissions at the state and federal level and translating

I am troubled by how many people see problems and remain silent. Too many take the attitude that "it's not my job" or are afraid to speak up. I call both leadership and people to account here. After all, there is no more important management principle than to "Drive out fear" (Deming) and too many people live in fear. Frankly, most of it is not real, only perceived. But the practical impact is the same. Good leaders do not allow fear to fester.

At the same time, more people need to act on things they think need improvement. In many cases they can change things in their current jobs (and prove it works) or speak out in a proactive, constructive manner. This may take some courage. After all, some will be rejected. But doing so is just not that hard.

Finally, if your management does rule through terror, it may be time to look for something else.

that somewhat arcane language into billing codes could be quite complex. And impactful—billions are at stake.

She wanted to create a competitive advantage for her company and wondered if offering customers some sort of "money back guarantee" would allow her to do so. But she didn't know how much such a guarantee would cost and without a solid measurement of the quality of data the company provided, there was no way to know.

Steve Hassmann, at Chevron, had a different problem. His group measured data quality, consistently seeing numbers in the "high 90s." That seemed pretty good. Similarly, there were plenty of ongoing clean-up projects. So the data should have been pretty good.

Yet Hassmann noticed that concerns about data quality came up in every conversation with his peers. Planning an oil well, ensuring a crew was qualified, or evaluating performance all depended on data and people just didn't seem to trust whatever they used. He couldn't square the apparent good work and results with the day-in, day-out problems. What was going on?

## PROVOCATEURS DIG DEEPER

Potential provocateurs first need some hard facts to determine whether they have a problem and, if so, to guide initial improvements. Bob Pautke, as will be discussed in Chapter 9, tracked 20 records and Steve Hassmann looked at existing metrics in a different way. Both found problems.

When hard facts are not readily available, potential provocateurs should employ the Friday Afternoon Measurement and rule of ten, as discussed in Chapter 2. They'll provide quick, defensible first looks, often more than enough to motivate further action.

## PROVOCATEURS ACHIEVE A REAL RESULT

Having found a worthy problem, provocateurs keep an open mind to new ways to address it and demonstrate they can tackle at least part of it.

As they gain traction on the problem, they tend to move quickly and keep the focus narrow, aiming for concrete results (note these actions represent the first two of the three phases of a data quality program – gaining traction and getting the first real results).

In Fleming's case, the obvious solution was to make a "more golden" copy. He could buy more sources or invest in better algorithms for selecting better data. Instead he decided to try the getting in front approach with one market data provider for one type of data. He picked a friendly one (Interactive Data), explained his thinking, and asked Interactive to measure the quality of data as he saw it using a variant of the Friday Afternoon Measurement. Conventional wisdom at the time was that market data providers held all of the leverage and were uninterested in working with individual banks. This turned out not to be the case at all—Interactive found plenty of reasons to work with Fleming and his team.[29]

Constructive work followed (and the usual posturing decreased) as Fleming and his team learned what it took to be a good customer, Interactive learned how to make measurements against their requirements, and a cross-company team selected improvement opportunities, usually opting for small projects that they could complete quickly. All told, it took about nine months for Fleming to demonstrate real results.

There were three big insights for Russo and her team. The first came as Stephanie Fetchen constructed a data quality metric and looked at monthly results for the previous year. Nine months were quite good, two were pretty bad, and one was absolutely terrible. Their process for creating tariff data was, quite simply, out of

---

[29] I told this story through Interactive's eyes in *Data Driven*.

control. Whether they offered a rebate or not, they had to fix that first. Sorting out the reasons for out-of-control situations, establishing countermeasures, and developing and rolling out needed training took about a year, all told.

> Provocateurs move as quickly as they can to gain traction and achieve their first real results. Two opposing forces here: First, the narrower the focus, the faster they can go. But the result has to be "real," meaning large enough that others respect it. It usually doesn't take long to have a good idea and you should expect to see positive signs in a few months. Finally, push for a real result in a year or less.

The second insight was that a rebate wouldn't do the Tele-Tech customers, usually big telecoms, any good. Any rebate was tiny compared to the problems errors caused. Customers simply wanted the data to be correct. So instead of offering a rebate, they decided to offer a cookie—any person who reported an error got their choice of chocolate chip or oatmeal raisin. Just enough of a reward, and a fun one at that, that people would actually report errors.

Third, they decided that they and their competitors talked about how good their data was, but none had done anything to prove it. So Fetchen and Russo decided to publish monthly DQ stats, warts and all! Customers could see the facts right there in the monthly report.

For Hassmann, a light came on when he dug into the data quality metric his department used. He saw two things: First, that the selected metric made the data look a lot better than it was. Second, clean-ups notwithstanding, the sheer volume of erroneous data was growing. Sorting this out convinced him that he had to get in front of the problem. So he decided to put a Data Quality Team, dedicated to doing just that, in place. He didn't rush this step. He had a particular manager (Nikki Chang) in mind and waited until she could join his team. Then he demanded rapid progress, across all Chevron companies, on a selected category of data. This required Chang to put embedded data managers in those companies, train them on quality management, track progress, and help them solve particularly challenging problems. All told, it took about a year to achieve the first real results.

## PROVOCATEURS ARE NOT RABBLE ROUSERS

The term "provocateurs" may conjure an image of angry young men and women, malcontents, free spirits, iconoclasts, or rabble rousers, unable to work within a corporate structure and always thinking out-of-the-box. I find that characterization completely wrong. The ones I've known were simply trying to improve their teams and their work. They may be dissatisfied with bureaucracy, feel impatient with the status quo, or have an idea that they want to try. But they're terrific corporate citizens, working as best they can to do what's best for their teams and companies. Their first choice is to work within the existing corporate framework.

It can be especially difficult to push forward when you think doing so is contrary to the boss's wishes. For example, Samantha, the rising star in Chapter 2, explicitly told her subordinate Steve to "check those numbers from the Widget department every time." Steve, having attended a quality class and determining there is a better way, may feel hard-pressed to propose working proactively with the Widget department on data quality to his boss.

But he must! He must realize that she hadn't given the subject any thought. In this case, she even made her statement at a time of great emotion. Bosses deserve to hear people's best ideas, even when those ideas may conflict with something the boss said at one time. Everyone should be a provocateur from time to time.

This is not to excuse bosses from their obligations to drive out fear. And people must show some courage!

Those I've worked with have been reasonably politically savvy. They keep their bosses informed (even try to make their bosses look good) and they seek buy-in from all involved in their early efforts. They have a sense of urgency and they persist, not easily frustrated by mistakes or failures along the way. They learn from these experiences and move on. They tend to be good cheerleaders, giving ample credit to everyone involved in the work and celebrating success.

## PROVOCATEURS HAVE COURAGE AND JUDGMENT

What distinguishes provocateurs from others is courage. It takes courage to look deeply into something that nearly everyone else accepts. Those hidden data factories are great examples. Most people have come to believe that they are needed, work well, and are the only real choice. Even taking a deep look requires more courage than many will muster.

It takes even more courage to point out the shortcomings. After all, people and the organization have a lot of money and ego invested in those hidden factories. And it is so easy to succumb to the mentality "Better to keep quiet — that's the way we've always done things around here."

Finally, it takes courage to try something new. The cold, brutal reality is that most new ideas fail and many perceive that it is better to not try anything than to be tied to a failure. Besides, it is easy enough to stand on the sidelines, opining that "someone should do something about this," while refusing to engage in a meaningful way.

One reason that provocateurs are courageous is that they see risk and opportunity more holistically. To illustrate, consider a problem that is costing a company $10 million a year. Someone develops a potential solution that has a 50 percent chance of success at a cost of $1 million. It is easy to see the downside, "There is a 50 percent chance of failure and I'll be blamed for costing the company a million dollars."

Provocateurs focus on the upside, "There's a 50 percent chance I can save the company $10 million a year."

Provocateurs show good judgment. In the situation above, they'll find a way to invest that million dollars in $100,000 increments, each time getting a better sense of the probability of success and adjusting course to better the odds.

When they enroll others in their work, as they must do at some point, provocateurs acknowledge that people have seen plenty of grand corporate efforts come and go. They acknowledge the risk that others perceive in the data quality effort, and they help people work through these concerns. Provocateurs explain to their collaborators that this is slow, patient work. It takes far more effort than anyone can imagine. But there is no substitute.

**Instructions:**

The instructions for becoming a provocateur may seem impossibly abstract. Still, Figure 5.1 captures the essence.

Figure 5.1 A process that a potential provocateur can use to decide whether to proceed and, if so, to complete his or her role.

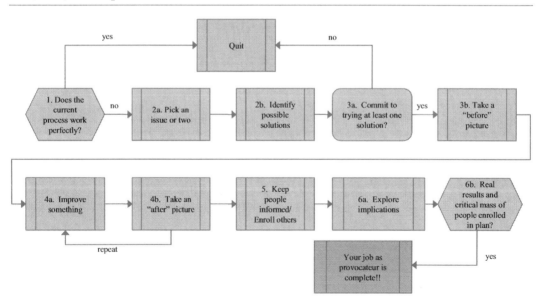

Steps 1 through 3 are for potential provocateurs:

1.   Ask questions about your current work and the associated processes:

    a. Are we operating a data factory, hidden or otherwise?

    b. Do we understand the needs of our most important customers?

    c. Can they trust the data we provide them?

    d. Are we positioned the way we want in the eyes of customers and prospects?

    e. Do we trust the data provided to us by others?

    f. Have we communicated our most important needs to our most important data creators (do we even know who they are)?

    g. Do we have the facts relevant to the quality of data we receive or provide? If not, gather some using the so-called Friday Afternoon Measurement.

    h. What is the essential value our current work provides? Is it worth the cost?

    i. Is the work improving fast enough in terms of quality, cost, and speed?

If everything about the current work is perfect, no need to go further.

2. Pick a couple of processes or steps that, when viewed properly, are simply broken. Dig deeper into each, asking why they are that way. Propose solutions, with a preference for faster, lower-budget, narrowly targeted approaches within your span of control, or influence.

3. Select two or three issues and proposed solutions from step 2 and decide whether to commit to seeing these solutions through (or not). If you commit, take a "before" picture, so you can later evaluate the impacts of your efforts.

And steps 4 through 6 are for those who commit:

4. Make an improvement (i.e., gain traction). This will usually involve working with data creators, customers, or inside your process to find and eliminate the root causes of error. Take an "after" picture and evaluate results, as non-judgmentally as you can. Continue in this fashion (adjusting as you go) until you have a real result. Move quickly!

5.  Maintain a proper balance, keeping people informed and enrolling them in the effort. At the same time, don't promise more than you are certain you will deliver.

6.  Explore the implications. Develop a mental image of "the world as it could be" and sort out a long-term plan. Your work as a provocateur is done when a critical mass of people understand these implications and plan.

## In Summary

My fondest hope for this book is that it will stimulate more people to become provocateurs. There are plenty of opportunities and it is not so hard. I know that becoming a provocateur seems scary. But, there is nothing more satisfying than putting the ball in motion as part of an effort that will fundamentally alter your team's (and maybe your company's) future.

# CHAPTER 6
## Building a Data Quality Team

In a perfect world, data customers and data creators reach out to one another. Customers clarify their needs, data creators work hard to meet them, and hidden data factories shrink. And people, energized by data they understand and trust, find new and creative ways to use it. They improve existing products, dream up new ones, and make the occasional "this changes everything" discovery. Life is wonderful in the data quality space.

Of course reality is far tougher and more confusing. While customers and creators can reach out to one another, relatively few do. Inertia reigns as too many remain comfortably isolated in their silos. As I've already noted, most know the data they use isn't very good, but they accept it as a fact of life. Far too many people assume that data is the province of the IT department and so don't give their roles as data creators and data customers much thought. Provocateurs may well have stimulated innovation at the work team or department level, but people conclude the example isn't relevant to them. So consolidating the gains and getting to the next level is tough. Finally, there is the age-old complaint that "my management doesn't get it." It is a weak excuse, but a barrier to progress nonetheless.

This is where data quality management comes in. I sometimes say that the whole point of data quality management is to connect data customers and data creators. It's a bit simplistic, but it does get to the heart of the matter. The vast majority of data

> Said differently, if the provocateur's work has covered "some customers," or "some data," the data quality team's role is to address "all important customers" or "all important data" at the department or company level.

customers will come out of their silos and almost all creators will work hard to satisfy customers—when given sufficient reason to do so. Thus, if a provocateur's efforts have led to the *first real results*, the goal of a department level quality team, in concert with more senior management (next chapter), is to *get to the next level*. The quality team is one subject of this chapter.

There are at least two areas, the corporate data definitions and "proprietary data" (more about proprietary data in just a moment) that must be owned at the corporate level, in large companies anyway. Thus, large companies often need a corporate data quality team also. This team is the second subject of this chapter.

The instructions herein are aimed specifically at departmental and corporate data quality team leaders and, to lesser degrees, their teams and their bosses. I've chosen the word "leader" (as opposed to say, "manager" or "head") purposefully. My working definition of leader is "he or she who is out in front" and the thrust of the role is to provide the day-in, day-out leadership needed to advance data quality across a department and company, respectively.

Before summarizing the instructions, I want to expand on the circumstances in which most departmental and corporate data teams find themselves. First, the good news: They exist because some senior manager (perhaps three regimes ago) became convinced that one was needed. Often a provocateur has shown real results on which this senior executive wants to build. As discussed in Chapter 9, Monica Falkenthal knew that AT&T could not roll out its access program without one and Aera named "manage data and information" as one of its most important processes at its inception. So most data quality teams enjoy (or enjoyed at some point in the not too distant past) some level of support and mandate.

Now the bad news. For many, support is tepid and the mandate weak. For there is a wide gap between knowing you need something and knowing what it should do, how it should function, and helping it do its work. As a result, data quality programs that don't produce quickly are often good targets for budget reductions in tough times.

Further, while provocateurs, data customers, and data creators work within their spans of control (the difficulties in process management notwithstanding) data quality teams lead work outside their spans of control. The practical reality is they often must bring the less willing into the effort.

Lastly, everything about data quality is political. Even the most arcane topic can boil the blood: "Which country codes?" or "Whose data is better?" have provoked bloody political battles.

As a result, the DQ team leader's job involves starting a program with people over whom she has no control, on a larger scale, and in the face of brutal politics. She is a sort of enfeebled provocateur. Sounds like a great job!

But don't despair. The data quality team lead has the opportunity to make an unprecedented contribution, to radically alter his or her department's (company's) trajectory, and to change the culture for the better. This job is not for the faint of heart, but can

> You and your team should almost certainly not report to IT.

be great fun for the courageous, the persistent, and those excited about learning new things on the job, and quickly.

**Instructions:**

1. Make special provisions for proprietary data, which is uniquely your company's own and so provides the potential for sustained strategic advantage.

2. Focus the effort. Understand which data is most important. Start small, on a set of data or a business problem that everyone agrees is important. In time, expand to make sure the department (as a whole) has the high-quality data it needs to operate well (i.e., is a good data customer) and provides the data others need (i.e., is a good creator).

3. Engage more senior management. You need far more than moral support, so assign them concrete tasks.

4. Help others (including senior managers) understand their roles. Connect data creators and customers. You almost certainly need an aggressive training program to do so.

5.  Provide common functions (such as measurement) that make life easier for data creators.

6.  Own the data definition process.

7.  Actively manage change. Build and advance the business case for data quality.

8.  Build small, but powerful teams. Build a network of embedded data managers to help you gain leverage. Support their work. Encourage a few to become world class data quality professionals.

## PAY SPECIAL ATTENTION TO PROPRIETARY DATA

There is one category of data, proprietary, that is so important that it must be aggressively managed at the corporate level.[30] I use the term "proprietary data" after the 2003 *HBR* classic, "IT Doesn't Matter," by Nicholas Carr.[31] There, he introduced the contrasting notions of infrastructure and proprietary technologies. An infrastructure technology diffuses throughout the economy in support of numerous industries and, in time, becomes available to all. The electric grid and the railroad are classic examples. And most information technologies also fall into this category. It is difficult to sustain a competitive advantage via infrastructure technologies.

Proprietary technologies, on the other hand, can be protected, at least for a significant time. A patented drug and deep understanding of a sophisticated process are good examples. Because they are protected, their owners can gain and sustain a strategic (or competitive) advantage.

---

[30] In *Data Driven*, I pointed out that an organization's data is uniquely its own. Later, I expanded on the idea in "Invest in Proprietary Data for Competitive Advantage," March 28, 2013, http://blogs.hbr.org/2013/03/invest-in-proprietary-data-for/. Tom Davenport and I pushed the idea to its logical conclusion in "Getting Advantage from Proprietary Data," March 11, 2015, http://mobile.blogs.wsj.com/cio/2015/03/11/getting-advantage-from-proprietary-data/.

[31] Nicholas Carr, "IT Doesn't Matter," *Harvard Business Review*, May 2003, https://hbr.org/2003/05/it-doesnt-matter.

This thinking applies directly to data. Data earns proprietary status in two distinct ways — through completely unique data structures (e.g., definitions) and through content no one else has. Unique data structures probably offer the best long-term prospects. For example, Facebook and LinkedIn have found ways to gather interesting data about people through their *friends* and *connections*, respectively, and secured an advantage. Others don't have access to this data and network lock-in may help them maintain this advantage for some time. Another example is the CUSIP, a means of identifying securities and process trades efficiently. It is owned by the American Bankers Association and administered by Standard & Poor's and has provided a long-term advantage to S&P.

> Nearly 30 years ago, Stephen Brand made a prescient observation about the unfolding data revolution: "On the one hand, information wants to be expensive, because it's so valuable. The right information in the right place just changes your life. On the other hand, information wants to be free, because the cost of getting it out is getting lower and lower all of the time. So you have these two fighting against each other."
>
> This assessment is spot on. Data promises new value from insights that lead to better-targeted advertising, to ideas for new products, to "this changes everything" discoveries — the "expensive" half of Brand's observations. But unless you can create and protect a measure of proprietary data, you'll spend most of your life on the "free side." You probably don't need a lot of proprietary data. Just enough to distance yourself from the other guy.

Even without a proprietary data structure, companies should still seek to create advantage through their content. After all, only you have the specific transaction, "John Smith bought peas, bread, and grape Nehi at 9:27 AM on March 11, 2016, paying with his debit card!" Some retailers, including Amazon, Kroger, and Safeway, are getting pretty good at using this data to tailor their advertising to John. Even better, they can combine John's transactions with millions of others to understand buying patterns, improve supply chains, and rearrange store layouts.

Now it is easier for competitors to copy your successes with transactional data. One retailer develops an insight into customer behavior and others

> While few companies are truly exploiting their proprietary data, I wish to be clear that, over the long term, I view it as their most important data.

follow suit. But don't avoid this avenue on that score alone. After all, you conduct transactions every day, enriching the base of things the competitor doesn't know each time. And there can be a solid advantage therein. For example, pharmacies build a patient's prescription history to better identify possible drug interactions, suggest cheaper generics, and get customers into their stores. It is no coincidence that patients must walk to the back to get to the pharmacy!

The key to exploiting proprietary data lies in identifying which offers the most potential for profit and sustained advantage. Thus, innovators may seek competitive advantage in their product and service data; the low-cost providers on operations and process data; and those aiming for customer intimacy on customer data.

With this background, it's clear enough that companies should manage proprietary data at the corporate level. While others will take the lead role in building proprietary data into products, the corporate DQ team lead must help identify this data and see that its gets the special attention it deserves. In particular, he or she must ensure that data creators recognize their special significance and improve them ceaselessly, make sure this data is clearly defined, look to extend the advantage by enriching this data, and keep them safe from the prying eyes of competitors and pirates. And, while the DQ team may not have revenue accountability, it should help those who do look for new ways to help put distance between yourselves and your competitors.

## FOCUS THE EFFORT

### Understand which data is most important

See Figure 6.1. The x-axis depicts the willingness of people to assume their roles as data creators and data customers. Close in are the willing, further out the less willing. The y-axis represents the criticality of all of the data the department either creates or uses.

Figure 6.1 The y-axis depicts criticality of a department's (corporation's) data along a continuum, from absolutely essential to never used by anyone. The x-axis depicts the willingness of people to participate as data creators and data customers, also along a continuum, from those showing leadership to subverters.

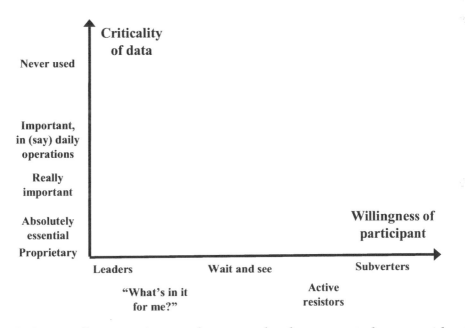

This axis is actually a continuum, but to make the concept clear, consider five categories:

1. **Proprietary**. Just discussed.

2. **Absolutely essential**. These are core to the department's mission, its management, or some external data customer and account for at most a few percent of all of the data.

> The DQ team lead should always be able to opine, "This data is most important to the department overall and here's why. Here's what's next and next after that. The DQ program addresses, or will address these, in the following ways…"

3. **Really important**. The department will be hard pressed to carry on without this data. Perhaps 3 to 5 percent of all data.

4. **Important**. The department needs it to function day-to-day, make routine management decisions, and fulfill corporate obligations. All data that leaves the department, if they don't fall into any of the categories above, are important.

5. **No one ever uses it**. I'm virtually certain at least 50 percent of all data falls into this category.

In time, the DQ team must sort out which data falls into each category. Doing so requires a deep understanding of the department, the data it uses and creates and the data it passes on to others. The work involves a large synthesis of the needs of

> From time to time, in public settings, I claim that as much as "90 percent of the data is never used for anything by anyone. Ever. Exclamation point!" So far, the only people who've challenged me claim my number is too low.

both departmental customers and the department's customers. The "most important data" rankings can, and should, change in time. A healthy department brings in new kinds of data regularly, shifts its priorities, grows, and takes on new roles, all requiring occasional adjustment to the ranking. Done well though, the most important data rankings should change pretty slowly (unless there are major changes to the department's mission) and serve the DQ team lead for years.

### Start with something everyone agrees is important

I find the experiences of Nikki Chang, in her first year as team lead for the Drilling and Completions Department at Chevron, especially instructive. To set the scene, drilling a well is a complicated undertaking. You have to figure out where to drill, acquire all needed permits, schedule a rig, do the work (often running into unexpected surprises under earth and sea), make the well ready for production, and accomplish all this safely and efficiently. Drilling and Completions both creates and uses massive quantities of data to do its work.

Further, the "department" is a sort of confederation of parts of Chevron business units, each operating in its own geography, drilling through different geologies, and under different regulatory constraints.

After talking to lots of people, Chang decided to start her program with "well header data" and to include all business units. While not everyone would agree that well header is the absolutely most essential, no one would deny it was really important. Further, the associated data is small and well-understood—she and others could focus their efforts as they learned what it took to improve data quality. Finally, these two points would help her secure the support of the business units.

Chang asked business units to do two things: First, to name an embedded data manager (which she called a "responsible coordinator") with whom she and her team could work. Second, to pursue a 95 percent target, for newly-created data within year-end. Finally, Chang set up her team to help business units reach the target. She explicitly did not tell business units how to do so, (after all she did not own their processes) but measured their progress, shared success stories, and supported them in numerous ways.

As she was gaining experience, Chang also sorted out her long-term program, effectively a plan for bringing all of Drilling and Completions into the fold.

## Craft a long-term plan

In time, of course, the DQ program should extend to all important data, customers and creators. Conceptually, you're choosing a sequence of phases that cover the required space, as depicted in Figure 6.2.

Figure 6.2 Craft the data quality program as a series of phases, eventually tackling as much important data as possible. To do so, you must silence subverters and active resistors and turn those adopting a wait-and-see attitude into willing participants.

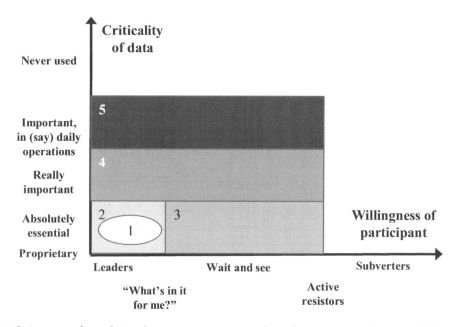

The trick is to craft and implement a program that does so, starting small, learning (and teaching) as you go, building capability, helping more and more people understand their roles as data creators and customers, and shepherding the program along. Sometimes the choice is easy—proceed from more costly to less-costly errors and bring people in as you go. In other cases, it may be better to proceed on the x-axis. You don't want the unwilling as part of your program— they'll take up too much of your time and deliver poor results. Instead, focus on turning the "wait and sees" into "what's in it for me's" and the "what's in it for me's" into the "leaders." Having senior management on your side can help do so!

More generally, aim to gain traction within four to six months and to show real results with the completion of Phase 1 in no more than a year. Phase 2 should cement your program as here to stay—you've reached the "next level." There's still plenty of work to do of course. But you've demonstrated success, built a competent staff, and solidified senior management's help (just below). You've arrived!

## ENGAGE SENIOR MANAGEMENT

Data quality programs go as far and as fast as the senior manager (or group of senior managers) perceived to be leading the effort demands. You need your department head to (appear to be) fully engaged. Better still, his or her entire staff. To be clear, "support" is not enough.

I noted earlier that too many people claim their management "doesn't get it" when it comes to data quality. It is contrary to my experience. Every single senior manager I've worked with has been smart—really, really smart. If they don't get it, chances are high no one ever explained it to them properly. Further, what exactly in a senior manager's past would enable him or her to "get" data quality? The notion of creating data correctly the first time is easy enough, but relatively few have heard of it.

Exacerbating this, many managers have had bad experiences

Recall my discussion with a senior media executive to start Chapter 1: "Did you trust the data you used to make your last important decision?" It made data quality personal, and aimed to engage both heart and head. I've yet to meet a senior executive who fully trusted budget, staffing, and sales reports that he or she relies every day. So this should be an easy conversation.

Conversely, I've not met a senior manager who cared how many ways IBM was expressed in the customer database, or about the pure error rate. If you think that way, you're going to send an easy conversation in the wrong direction.

with those promoting quality. They've been subjected to such demotivating lines as:

*"We examined 5,437,124 customer data records and 271,356 of them had errors in the address field. This demands our immediate attention."*

*"In just the financial systems alone, we have 42 ways of recording IBM. Don't you think we ought to do something about it?"*

They've been through endless rounds of data clean-up. Worse, the problems seem so esoteric and the proposed solutions so complex.

Finally, my experience has been that most senior managers know, deep down, that data quality is an issue. They want to help, but they don't know what to do. Again, how exactly would they know? Who is advising them on these matters, helping them understand how data quality should fit in their departments, sifting through the extravagant claims, setting a practical course of action, and, as much an anything else, understand their roles?

The only plausible answer to these two questions is "the DQ team lead."

To be clear here, do not ask your senior management to *support* the data quality program. Support is too vague. Give them specific tasks and help them complete those tasks. Here are some examples. Ask them:

1. To speak, in their own words, about the importance of high-quality data in town halls and other meetings. Coach them to do so effectively.
2. To make time in staff meetings for you to instruct the management team on their roles as data customers and creators.
3. To make personal statements about the importance of each phase of the data quality effort.
4. To introduce you to people you need to know to do your job effectively.
5. To write articles for their quarterly newsletters. Give them draft text.
6. To appear in videos you use to promote data quality awareness. Coach them.

7. To be your personal mentor, advising you on opportunities and risks along the way.

8. To recognize individuals who've done something exceptional when it comes to data quality.

9. In time, to include quality goals in yearly planning efforts.

10. In time, to include data quality targets in performance contracts and reviews.

Excuse my naked advertisement here, but outsiders can often help engage senior management in ways that insiders can't. Don't be territorial in this respect—you need to engage your senior management. Do so by any means at your disposal.

This list can go on and on. As they grow comfortable, good managers will provide the leadership you need without being asked. That's when you know you've succeeded in this task. Then redouble your efforts and move quickly. Good times don't last forever.

## CONNECT DATA CREATORS AND DATA CUSTOMERS

As you work through each phase, you must connect the relevant data customers and data creators. This is demanding, sometimes frustrating, work and unfortunately I know of no way to make it easier. I prefer to start with customers. Facilitate a customer's needs workshop and help relevant customer groups complete the documentation (alternatively, put together a short class on the topic). Coach customers, especially those who are just beginning to recognize their roles as customers, how to communicate their needs.

Next work with data suppliers. You may have to work backwards through a series of data warehouses, transactional systems, and other technologies to sort out who the data creators are. Get as close as you can. Then arrange meetings between the two. In the short term, your goal is to get the two parties talking. Longer term, you're building communication channels. You'll know you've succeeded when the two sides talk regularly without your involvement.

Your job isn't complete until the data creator agrees to take steps to improve and knows how to do so. Note your overlapping roles, helping people and teams see themselves as data creators and customers, teaching them what to do, and facilitating their connection.

One final instruction: These early engagements are a perfect time to build support for the notion of an embedded data manager. As you connect the two, ask that each side name someone to assume primary responsibility for the relationship going forward. Whether in name only, this person has taken on some of the responsibilities of the embedded data manager. Give this person special attention, extol the virtues of the role, and look for opportunities to formalize it.

## PROVIDE COMMON FUNCTIONS WHERE IT MAKES SENSE

Data quality teams often perform four common functions:

- Measurement.
- Data supplier management, on behalf of data customers, for common suppliers.
- Training of data creators, data customers, and more senior management.
- Establishing standard measurement, control, and other methodologies at the corporate level.

In Chevron, for example, 15 business units all create well header data. It would involve 15 times as much effort for each to develop and manage its own measurement function. Worse, each could

> Many procurement groups have extensive teams related to product quality but miss data altogether (then complain that the data isn't up to snuff). Further, I find that most external suppliers will engage on data quality quite readily—far more readily that internal departments. DQ teams should exploit this opportunity!

come up with similar but not comparable measurements. Finally, measuring data quality at Chevron is quite technical, beyond the easy reach of many creators, so Nikki Chang's group does the measurement work for all. Of course, Chang must measure data quality to manage her program.

In the same vein, some of the data that ranks "important or above," is created outside the company and DQ team leads (usually at the corporate level) must bring them into the fold. In some cases, a DQ team member should lead the engagement. In others, it is sufficient to include terms related to data quality in contracts. DQ teams should encourage the procurement department to set up its own data quality team or at least staff the embedded data manager role.

Finally, training is a must. I've already discussed the importance of training senior management. Beyond that, since everyone is both a data customer and creator, they ought to receive enough training to participate in meaningful ways (say participating in improvement projects and contributing to customer needs). Embedded data managers need considerably more, and a few specialists need in-depth training. A good role model in this regard is Shell Finance, where Ken Self led development and delivery of a curriculum consisting of:[32]

- *Data Quality Awareness*: A video for all that highlights the main points.
- *Data Quality and You*: A six-workshop sequence that guides embedded data quality managers and specialists in applying the tasks discussed in the previous two chapters in the context of their jobs.
- *The Manager's Course in Data Quality*: A two-session workshop that asks managers to apply data quality in their work.
- Deeper, computer-based training for members of data quality teams.

These specifics aside, I rarely advocate for centralization of the day-in, day-out work of data quality management. The issue is simple: centralizing the work makes it appear that the data quality team, not data customers and data creators,

---

[32] Andy Koronois, Ken Self, and Thomas Redman, "On-the-Job Data Quality Training at Shell Finance," *IAIDQ Newsletter*, October 2012, http://iaidq.org/publications/doc/koronios-2012-08.shtml.

is responsible for data quality. To lay this bare, consider controls. As discussed in Chapter 4, good controls play a big role in data quality. But there are many types of controls, some quite technical and data customers usually have some, in the form of a hidden data factory. Wouldn't it be better to have some central team (say the data quality team) operate those controls? Doing so would save money. And customers would see fewer errors.

A seductive trap indeed! Bringing the hidden data factory into the light and doing the work well is indeed a step up. But the benefits pale in comparison to getting responsibility for data where it belongs, with data creators and data customers.

Don't fall into this trap. Your job is to lead the data quality effort, not run a hidden data factory to clean up bad data left by those who don't do their jobs. Provide common functions where it makes sense, but insist that data customers and creators step into their roles.

## OWN THE DATA DEFINITION PROCESSES

Data quality team leads should own the data definition process discussed in Chapter 4. Ideally, most of this work is led at the corporate level, and departmental level work fills in gaps. There may well be many such gaps, as your department almost certainly employs specialized language—terms used widely within your department, though of little interest to most others.

## ACTIVELY MANAGE CHANGE

One could argue that the DQ Team's job is change management and that all of the tasks discussed so far, and the organization, discussed next, simply support that job. The argument would point out that the essence of the role is changing the culture—getting people to recognize and take on roles as data creators and data customers, in the face of organizational momentum and office politics. Further, while the same issues come up over and over, all politics is local. So the argument is sound.

I know of no simple "cookbook-style" instruction for managing change. Still, the following will help.

First, build the case for data quality that engages both the "head and heart." By the head, I mean the sober analysis of cost reduction and other tangible business benefits laid out in Chapter 2. By the heart, I mean the organization's deeply held values, the things that cause an emotional reaction. Thus, in a hospital "We've got to improve data quality because bad data kills" will get far more attention than "We've got to improve data quality because laboratory errors cost us an average of $117 to correct."

I find that all good organizations have values, from taking care of patients to commitment to low prices to innovation and even to year-end bonuses. Data quality programs that expose a threat to, or the opportunity to advance, these values have a leg up.

In a similar vein, craft your program to build on the organization's strengths. Thus, play up the measurement aspects in organizations with good quantitative skills; play up control in top-driven command and control organizations; play up cross-departmental improvement projects in organizations that view teamwork as a strength.

Second, communicate, communicate, communicate. Publicize successes, recognize those who've led improvement projects, put articles in newsletters, be transparent about your plans, and on and on. Allot plenty of time for this work. As a rule of thumb, follow this algorithm:

To estimate how much effort you must devote to communication:

> **Step 1:** Estimate how much effort you should devote to communication.
> **Step 2:** Multiply by ten.

Third, there are plenty of great models for managing change. Figure 6.3 presents a simple model I use to help clients craft their change management plans. If you've already got something you like, use it. If not, give this one a try.

Lastly, and perhaps most importantly, have a real success in Phase 1 before you start bragging. Too many programs start with a high-minded, "It's gonna be great" advertisement.

Your communications will be far more powerful when they are of the form, "Look what the XYZ team accomplished. They had to learn some new skills along the way and it was a lot of hard work. They did it by focusing on eliminating some fairly basic errors, improving customer satisfaction and saving some real money along the way. Of course we're all different. But their story ought to be the standard for our department."

Figure 6.3: I learned this model when I was at AT&T over 20 years ago (I don't recall ever knowing the source). It posits that four elements must *simultaneously* be in place if a change initiative is going to succeed.

Use these four elements to rate where you stand and improve your change efforts:

- *Sense of urgency.* Essentially you have to answer the question, "Why is data quality deserving of my time and attention, given I'm already working too hard?"
- *Clear, shared vision.* You have to answer the question, "If I do the things you're asking, what is the new world going to look like? How will it be better, ideally for me, but at least for something I care about?"
- *Actionable first step.* You have to answer the question, "So what do you want me to do differently tomorrow morning at 8:00AM, after I get my coffee?"
- *Capacity to change.* You have to make sure (or provide) people have the time, knowledge or training, financial resources, and emotional capacity to actually contribute.

## BUILD SMALL BUT POWERFUL CORE DATA QUALITY TEAMS

Figures 6.4 and 6.5 present the organization charts for the departmental and the corporate data quality teams respectively. Each sub team carries out some of the instructions given herein. The two charts are quite similar, reflecting (largely) common objectives, just at different levels. The biggest differences are the team focused on proprietary data and common data definitions, at the corporate level. And, as previously expressed, "small but mighty" is the goal in both cases.

Figure 6.4 Proposed organization structure for a departmental data quality group.

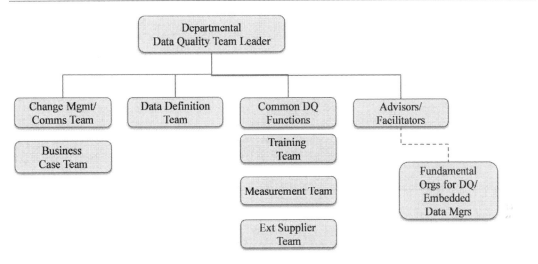

Figure 6.5 Proposed organization structure for a corporate data quality group.

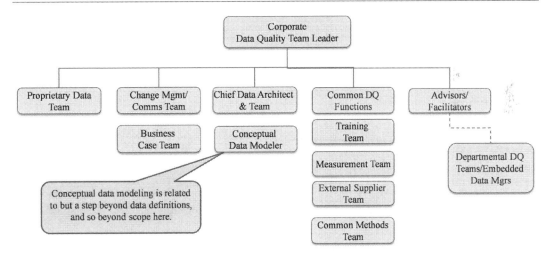

## Build a network of embedded data managers and team leads

One of the recurring themes of this book is that the actual work of data quality management is completed "close to the ground," where people actually create and use data.

This point underscores the importance of building a network of data quality professionals, specifically the data managers embedded in the work. Work with management to put them in place as you proceed through the phases or your program, train them, and help them in any way you can.

> I generally prefer to decentralize, putting embedded data managers in the line. This may not be appropriate early on, before they have skills, experience, and confidence. It's okay that for them to report into the DQ Team for a time. Get them into the line as soon as you can.

Similarly, corporate team leads must establish a network of departmental data groups and work through them wherever possible.

### Develop a few world-class data quality professionals

Companies that hope to effectively exploit their data need a couple of world class data quality professionals, people with wide experience and expertise in all things related to data quality. They are professionals who have the wisdom to put data quality in context, the courage to lead, the gravitas to prevail in difficult political situations, the depth of understanding and intellect to work out new solutions to problems beyond those discussed here, and the vision to see opportunity. They are people who wish to make data quality their life-long profession. I call such people "data maestros."

> Good companies always take steps to identify and nurture rare professional talent. For data quality, it is complicated by the fact that "data quality professional" does not yet have the same allure as, say, "petroleum engineer."

There are relatively few data maestros out there. Even if you can attract one to your company, you need to develop more. Identify candidates early and set them on aggressive paths. Give them a variety of on-the-job experiences (including as embedded data managers), send them to conferences and external training, encourage them to read everything in sight, and get them a mentor with expertise in the field. This will take time and it is easily subverted by the pressures of the day. But these people are the future, so keep this high on your priority list.

## In Summary

Your department and company need high-quality data. Your job is to see they get it. Further, it is always in your company's interest to make sure that data delivered to customers, potential customers, regulators, and others is of high-quality. It is just plain smart to minimize hidden data factories between departments. Data quality teams, including embedded data managers, bear day-in, day-out responsibility for making this happen. It takes leadership, planning, political acumen, and hard work, day-in and day-out. The job can be frustrating and, simultaneously, the most rewarding experience ever. You have a unique opportunity to make your department and company stronger.

Table 6.1 Data quality team indicators of success.

| You've | When |
|---|---|
| Gained Traction | Hopefully you are able to build upon the success of a provocateur. Whether this is the case or not, you've lined up a "Phased" effort, successfully understood the needs of one important customer, connected that customer to an important data creator, made a measurement against those needs, and seen at least one real improvement. |
| Achieved Real Results | You've completed a legitimate Phase 1 effort on proprietary, essential, or important data; featuring several improvement projects making a real difference for at least one customer. You've gained some experience, including with an embedded data manager. |
| Make it to the Next Level | You've laid out a long-term program, completed a second Phase, are well along in building a powerful team, and have brought senior management into your program. You're far from done, but the needed changes are beginning to take hold. |

# CHAPTER 7
## Essential Roles of Senior Management in Getting to the Next Level

This chapter is aimed at senior departmental and corporate managers. It is motivated by my earlier observation that data quality programs go as far and as fast as the senior manager (or management team) perceived to be leading the effort insists. This doesn't mean that provocateurs cannot achieve a real result or two, or that data quality teams without strong mandates can't make progress. They can, and they do, all of the time.

But the overall program reaches a plateau and after that progress is too slow and uncertain. Further, you're lucky if one person in 500 has the insight, courage, wisdom, and persistence to be an effective provocateur–far too few for data quality to permeate the entire organization.

If you want your entire department or company to enjoy the benefits of high-quality data, then you must actively engage. Some 20 years ago, Dr. Joseph Juran, captured this cold, brutal reality brilliantly, making the case that leadership for quality cannot be delegated.[33] While Juran was talking about manufacturing quality, his words ring true for data as well. If anything the data quality challenge is tougher.

You must insist that your organization get in front on data quality and, in so doing, close those wasteful hidden data factories; you must put the right people and organizational structure in place; and over time, you must make clear that contributing to the effort is not optional. Your efforts need not take a lot of your time, but they must be genuine, consistent, long-term, and forceful.

---

[33] Joseph Juran, "Made in USA: A Renaissance in Quality," July 1993, https://hbr.org/ product/made-in-u-s-a-a-renaissance-in-quality/93404-PDF-ENG.

**Instructions:**

1. Develop a feel for the issues as they impact you personally. Understand the case for data quality and what you must do. Then decide: go for it or not.

2. Put a data-friendly structure and the right people in place. Adopt a federated model for managing data quality and get the right people in corporate and departmental lead roles. Don't look to IT to lead the DQ effort.

3. Build the culture. Insist that your department or company get in front on data quality. Set high targets for the DQ team and your organization.

4. Actively engage.

## UNDERSTAND THE BUSINESS CASE

I started this book recounting a discussion I had with a senior media executive as he tried to understand what data quality meant. He resonated when I asked whether he trusted the data the last time he made an important decision (he couldn't recall ever fully trusting the data).

This example underscores an important point—it is easy to think of data quality as some esoteric problem buried in computers. Many data managers unwittingly reinforce the misconception! So senior managers should first consider how data quality affects them personally. Perhaps you too have been frustrated when you couldn't trust data needed for a big decision, perhaps you grew angry at a direct report when he or she "bent the truth" in describing a problem in his or her work, perhaps you were confused when three department heads gave you different numbers for last month's results, perhaps you felt enfeebled when they had no data whatsoever to address a new issue, perhaps you worried whether a similar error could happen to you after a colleague was called out in the news for a big mistake rooted in bad data.

This exercise can be tricky—we've all grown accustomed to excusing little issues and viewing more major ones as "just one of those things." Think through colleagues you work with and the sources in your personal network, making mental notes of those you simply don't trust. Revisit important decisions, asking yourself how much of the data you considered turned out to be false, misleading, or otherwise not up to snuff. Look too at hidden data factories in your own work, things you and your staff do to accommodate bad data. Recall yourself as the rising star of Chapter 2. Now develop your own mental picture.

In parallel, develop the larger case for data quality. Include three components:

- Some deeper knowledge about how good the data really is.
- "So what?"—a better understanding of everything from day-in, day-out operations to the company's long-term strategies to the plans to "compete with data."
- Addressing the tough question, "do I want to put in the time and energy this will require?"

### How good is the data?

You can get the deeper facts by conducting a few Friday Afternoon Measurements (Chapter 2) and talking to colleagues. Interestingly, I find that (when in a non-threatening environment and encouraged to think it through) most senior managers readily admit that data causes plenty of grief and recall many specifics.

### So what?

You can estimate the hard costs associated with bad data by sorting out the costs of a hidden data factory or two and by employing the rule of ten (also Chapter 2). Expect numbers in the range of 20 to 50 percent or more of the total costs of operations.

Unfortunately, it is impossible (so far anyway) to associate hard costs with impacts such as:

- Missed opportunities.
- Bad decisions.

- Angered customers.
- Turf wars because people can't trust each other's data.
- Difficulties in executing longer-term strategies.

But estimable or not, these costs are real, and you must factor them into your business case.

To continue the so-what analysis, think more opportunistically. Think not in terms of reducing costs, but in terms of creating benefits. Ask specifically, "How would the company be better if the data was better?" Perhaps the company would enjoy less friction between departments; perhaps you could put some distance between yourself and your nearest competitor; perhaps you could better use the data to innovate. It may be trite to observe that data is inseparable from operations, day-in, day-out management, and strategy, but it is certainly true. When thinking this way, many see leverage in high-quality data. And the answer to the so-what question is not one big reason, but dozens of little ones.

> Note that I did not pose this question as, "Can we do anything about it?" None of the instructions discussed herein are all particularly difficult, so you certainly can. Now to be fair, taken together, the new roles represent a big culture change, though certainly not beyond reach of any good management team. Even in the harshest light, you certainly can!

### Competing with data

Whether you buy into the hype associated with big data, advanced analytics, "data is an asset," and the Internet of Things, data is growing more important. So sooner or later, every company must have a data strategy.[34] While a full discussion is beyond scope here, I do wish to synthesize points made earlier.

---

[34] I believe Eric Schmidt of Google first made this observation. But I have been unable to find a reference I trust.

First, while you may not think about it explicitly, you're already competing with data. Consider the enormous quantities of data you expose externally, to your prospects, customers, suppliers, competitors, financial markets, and regulators. Bad data can leave bad impressions, and long-lasting ones at that.

Second, recall the four basic strategies[35] for competing with data (Chapter 2):

1. Becoming data-driven.
2. Using Big Data and Advanced Analytics to innovate.
3. Providing new and better content.
4. Becoming the low-cost provider (by reducing costs associated with hidden data factories).

The first three depend on high-quality data and the fourth is nothing but data quality.

Third, in the short-term, at the very least, you must protect yourself from the likes of Uber, which is transforming an entire industry simply by capturing "I'm looking for a ride" with "I'm looking for a fare." Think an upstart can't threaten you? Be circumspect in this regard. Ignore data and data quality at your peril.

Fourth, having a measure of proprietary data, data that you have and no one else does, is key to long-term strategic advantage (discussed more fully in Chapter 5). Even if you're ready for a full-fledged data strategy, you should identify and focus first on proprietary data.

Two instructions are clear:

1. You must factor the longer-term strategy, even if not-fully formed, into the near-term case for data quality.
2. Over the longer-term, you must sort out a data strategy.

---

[35] Thomas Redman, "4 Business Models for the Data Age," May 20, 2015, https://hbr.org/2015/05/4-business-models-for-the-data-age.

### Are you up for it?

The final question, "Do I want to put in the time and energy this will require?" is tougher, especially in light of Dr. Juran's observation that leadership cannot be delegated. There are plenty of reasons to answer, "No." After all, you may have other priorities, wish to leave a legacy in a different way, or lack the energy to take on anything new, never mind data quality.

There are also plenty of reasons to say "Yes." Data quality is the most effective way to cut costs, and it can help your company be a tougher competitor. On a personal level, advancing data quality may help you distinguish yourself from your peers. Better data will certainly help you make better decisions. Finally, you may use data quality as a means to explore the joys and perils of data, as emerging assets.

> You may need some minimalist data quality program to respond to regulators, mollify customers, or keep costs from exploding. Just don't confuse such a program with serious effort.

I have no easy prescription for answering this question. Just take a hard look in the mirror. If you're up for it, great. If not, so be it.

Then synthesize the above. If the business case intrigues and you're up for it, then engage, following the instructions that follow. If you don't believe the business case, have a better opportunity, or are simply not up for it, then leave data quality for your successor.

## PUT THE RIGHT PEOPLE AND STRUCTURE IN PLACE

This book explores the roles of people, as data creators and customers, process owners, embedded data managers, data quality team leads, and leaders. This section builds on earlier chapters, proposing a federated structure for managing data quality, advising on how many people a full-fledged data program will take, exploring where DQ teams should report, and describing traits you should look for in DQ team leads.

### Adopt a federated model for data quality management

Take a look at Table 7.1. It proposes a federated model for managing data, along the lines of a federated model for managing people.

Table 7.1 A federated approach for managing data assets parallels the approach for managing other assets, such as people.

|  | **People Management** | **Data Assets** |
|---|---|---|
| **Senior Executive** | Usually one of the top few executives in the company. | In time a Chief Data Officer will become one of the top few executives. |
| **Corporate HQ** | Corporate succession; policy and administration. | Corporate metadata management; provisions for unique data; strategy; policy. |
| **Departmental Staff** | Help their units find the talent they need; on-board people. | Help their units become good data customers and creators; drive departmental data program; home for embedded data managers. |
| **Everyone** | Day-in, day-out people management; follow established HR processes. | Good data customers and creators; develop novel ways to compete with data. |

The left-hand column summarizes pertinent features of "people management," including a high-level leader, a headquarters group that sets and administers policy, and HR people seeded throughout and reporting into departments. Still, the most interesting feature is that HR does relatively little actual people management. That happens "in the line," as managers build teams, provide feedback, negotiate performance contracts, advance (or not) the organization's culture, and hundreds of smaller actions every day. And not just managers. Everyone contributes, as they seek to improve their skills, interact with each other

In my opinion, companies should manage data as professionally and aggressively as other things they view as assets. People and capital almost always qualify. While I could base Table 7.1 on either, I chose people because I see important analogies between "data" and "what's in people's heads." See *Data-Driven* for a discussion of the larger implications of treating data as an asset.

in professional (and not-so-professional ways), provide 360° feedback, and again, in hundreds of smaller actions every day.

Over time, you need to build something similar for data, as the right-hand column proposes. Analogous features for managing data, include a high-level leader (e.g., a Chief Data Officer), a data quality team at headquarters, and data quality teams in departments. The analogy extends to people and managers as well. After all, everyone touches data every day and so must take on their responsibilities as both data customers and data creators. And managers must take on special responsibilities to ensure that processes work well, and to build needed communications channels with data suppliers and customers.

Of course different companies employ different management styles. Some take a more "command and control" approach, others are more highly decentralized and so adopt a more decentralized approach. Match the degree of centralization for data to the degree of centralization your company uses for people.

### How many people?

Continuing this discussion, see Figure 7.1, which provides "stake in the ground" estimates of how many people a solid data quality program will require. Not surprisingly, the more critical data is to creating and maintaining strategic advantage and the greater the intensity of interesting data, the more people required. These estimates stem from three sources:

- The sizes of quality staffs at AT&T and Motorola when they were in their quality heydays and won Baldrige Awards.

- Discussions with companies on the sizes of staffs associated with other assets, capital (e.g., Finance) and people (HR). While my study is hardly random, I've received numbers as low as 1.5 percent and as high as 6 percent, though most answers cluster around "about 2 percent." To be clear, these estimates reflect the number of people in full-time staff roles (including embedded data managers). Of course, as Figure 7.1 notes, everyone bears some responsibility for both HR and money/physical property, just as all who touch data are both creators and customers.
- Experiences with those enjoying success with data quality.

Depending on the criticality of data to strategy and a company's "quantity of interesting data," numbers can range from as low as 1 percent to as high as 4 percent. For most, I recommend 2 percent as "getting started" number, with two-thirds to three-quarters of those in embedded data manager roles and the remainder in staff roles. If those shares seem high, compare it to the 50 percent of time people devote to the hidden data factory!

Figure 7.1 Percentage of people in staff and embedded data manager roles.

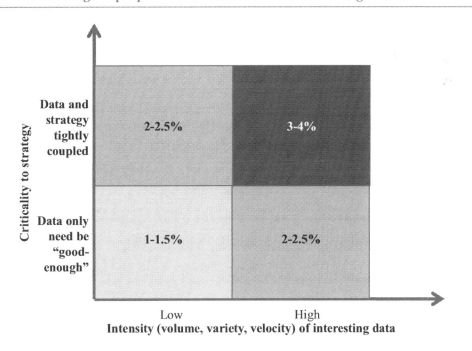

## Where should data teams report?

I've also noted herein that principle responsibility for data quality rests with data creators and data customers and that data quality teams should not report into IT. Rationale for this conclusion comes in two forms. Liz Kirscher, past president of the data business at Morningstar, explains it this way: "We would no more have Tech run data then we would have Research run Tech. They are different kinds of assets."[36]

> There was a time when the notion that data teams should report anywhere other than IT provoked some controversy. Today most IT departments readily admit that "the business owns the data."

Second is the fact that DQ teams reporting to Tech have not enjoyed the same levels of success as have teams reporting elsewhere. If your current data teams report into IT, find a better spot as quickly as possible.

Of course, "not in IT!" does not address the question of where the DQ Teams should report. For the corporate data team, my order of preference is as follows:

1. If you have a true Chief Data Officer (a lot of companies have CDOs, but relatively few are truly C-level jobs), then the DQ Team should report into him or her.

2. If you have no CDO, then to the CEO. I don't know of any companies doing this right now. But during the heyday of the quality movement in manufacturing, heads of Quality departments reported to CEOs, an arrangement that worked exceptionally well. In and of itself, data quality does not demand a C-level job. Depending on the size of the company, one or two levels down.

3. To either the Chief Operating Officer or Chief Financial Officer, whichever is better positioned to nurture the new area.

---

[36] Redman, Thomas C., "Data's Credibility Problem," *Harvard Business Review* December 2013.

This same logic applies for Departmental data teams. Get them as close to the department's most important data as you can, one or two levels below department head.

### Hire quick learners who aren't afraid to make mistakes

I've worked with many solid data quality team leads and I have three excellent ones in mind for this instruction on what to look for: Nikki Chang at Chevron, Karl Fleischmann at Shell, and Lwanga Yonke, at Aera Energy. First, look for someone who thinks independently and learns quickly. Fleischmann and Yonke, in particular are voracious readers. Chang questions everything. Look for someone who is already respected or can earn respect quickly. A deep understanding of your business is a real plus. Chang spent twenty years working on the information systems that support her unit, Fleischmann is a Ph.D. geologist, and Yonke has an advanced degree in petroleum engineering. All have huge networks and enjoy deep respect within their companies.

> Most companies, big ones anyway, need at least one world-class data quality expert. The practical reality is that you'll have to seek outside help until you develop or hire one.

Look for someone with the courage to take on sacred cows and the confidence to make mistakes. It is important to have some experience in data or quality, but fast learners pick it up quickly enough. A passion for data, and a dogged persistence are more important. Finally, look for extroverts. I find that the hard work of data quality is done in other people's offices, as one builds relationships, explains roles to people, helps solve problems and the like. While I've known some introverted data quality team leads, extroverts enjoy the role more.

## INSIST THAT THE ORGANIZATION GET IN FRONT ON DATA QUALITY

I find discussions about culture incredibly frustrating. People say things like "that's just a cultural issue" or "we have to change the culture first" as if those comments somehow clarified the matter. They don't, at least for me.

First, great companies already have great cultures, cultures of innovation, of service to customers, of citizenship, or commitment to people, and the like. Improved data can enhance those cultures. So attach data quality to values your company already holds dear.

Second, I've also noted several times that organizational momentum tends to

In Chapter 2, I used a rising star and her first presentation to the Board to show how hidden data factories come into existence. The essence of the story is that she learns of a critical error in data she obtains from another department, makes the correction, fails to inform the department responsible, and implements a process to check their numbers going forward (a hidden data factory). The question here is: If they know about this, what should her bosses do?

- One could argue that such things happen all of the time—indeed be glad she didn't sabotage the other department and forget about it.
- One could also argue that it is never okay to leave a colleague to be victimized—she should be shown the door!

Maybe it's the advisor in me, but I view this as a teachable moment. Heretofore, such behavior may have been acceptable, even the norm. But no longer. It is completely counter to getting in front on data and must stop.

relieve data creators of any responsibility for data quality. Data customers are pressed for time and they get immediate relief by making corrections, in time instantiating the effort in hidden data factories. Your biggest challenge lies in deflecting that momentum. No one will misunderstand the logic. But old habits die hard! You and your team leads must become "evangelists in chief" for the new approach to data quality.

Third, cultures are built on deeds, not words. Of course big things matter, but it's the dozens of little, unscripted things that leaders do that advance, or retard, the culture.

Fourth, there is a temptation to expand any cultural issue into a larger one. For example, many companies are struggling with what it means to be data-driven and you certainly can't become data-driven when you can't trust the data. Becoming data-driven sounds (to many) like a better rallying cry than "Let's fix the data," so sometimes this is a good idea.

Other times, not so much. People may find data-driven less tangible, while the data quality program provides specific to-dos and yields results more quickly. One solution is to look for a middle ground, along the following lines: "We want to become data-driven because doing so will enhance our existing culture. That's going to take a long time, as we learn exactly what that means and how we each contribute. In the short-term, let's focus on data quality. It's a bit more tangible and we've already had some big wins in the area." And in getting in front on data quality, we'll learn what it means to be data-driven.

### Focus the effort, setting stretch targets

Besides getting the right structure and people in place, the most helpful thing senior leaders can do for a data quality program is to create and sustain an urgency around the effort. This translates into narrowing the focus, measuring the quality of newly created data, and on setting demanding goals. As previously mentioned, I find that targets of the form, "Cut the error rate of XYZ in half every six months" highly effective. Depending on your circumstances, you may wish to adjust the time frame. In Liz Kirscher's case, at Morningstar, this meant halving the error rate every year, not six months. Conversely, halving the error rate every three months may be more appropriate for high-velocity data creation.

## ENGAGE VISIBLY

Perhaps nothing is more damaging to a data quality effort than a senior executive claiming publicly to be a whole-hearted supporter, then doing nothing.

All senior leaders know that to lead, you must be visible. This can feel uncomfortable when it comes to data, just as talking about anything new and unfamiliar can be.

In the last chapter, I advised DQ team leads to push their leaders to engage and provided them a list of ten opportunities. Obviously you need not do all ten. Pick a couple. As your confidence grows, I'm sure you'll think of plenty more.

The real purpose of this section is to propose that you take on two specifically. The first is this: Call for, then participate on, an improvement project. The next time someone gives you a report with an

A good deal of the benefit in a data policy stems from discussing the issues with senior management teams, sorting out where data and data quality fit, and, in some cases, clarifying the high-level flow of data across the company. The policy itself need do no more than clarify people's roles as data creators and data customers, e.g., "Don't take junk data from the last person. And don't send junk data on to the next person."

error in it, don't dismiss it. Rather, say, "Let's sort out what happened here, get to the root cause, and see that it doesn't happen again." Then be a full participant in the improvement team set up to do so. Two things will happen: First, you'll learn a lot about data, about becoming a good data customer, and about organizational issues that hinder data quality. Second, (as I'm sure you know) word will get out. Others will want to lead improvement projects also.

The second is a high-level policy that clarifies the management responsibilities described herein. The policy should be short, perhaps a page, and simply summarize what's expected of departmental leaders in advancing data quality and of everyone else in their roles as data customers and data creators.

## IN SUMMARY

Your department and company need high-quality data and it is always in your interest to make sure customers, potential customers, regulators, and others receive high-quality data. Further the data space is exploding in dozens of different directions. What today may be a strategic opportunity could well be a strategic imperative in just a few years and an all-out fight for survival a few more after that.

While provocateurs and DQ teams can achieve real results, data quality efforts plateau unless senior managers (at department and company levels) take responsibility for spreading the effort broadly and deeply. The steps you must take are quite obvious and, in any fair accounting, simpler than the alternatives of dealing with bad data. Still data quality requires a different mindset, new organizational constructs, and a culture shift. This is why you must engage.

# CHAPTER 8
## Great Data Quality Programs Need Great Tech

Tech departments are in tight spots when it comes to data quality. Many people automatically assume Tech is responsible for all things data. A sort of "if it's in the computer, it must be Tech" logic. But of course Tech is neither an important data creator nor customer, so it is singularly ill-positioned to do much about quality. Still, when the data doesn't meet their needs, people blame Tech.

Similarly, companies want to increase capacity and decrease costs by automating their business processes. But to paraphrase Dr. W. Edwards Deming: "Don't automate processes that produce junk. You'll just produce more junk faster."[37]

> This dynamic may take place with hidden data factories as well. A department or company recognizes it has an ineffective data factory and asks Tech to automate it. Results do not satisfy. And Tech gets blamed.

While Dr. Deming was talking about factory automation, his words are no less true for computers and data. Automating a broken business process just produces more bad data. Companies made this mistake over and over. Then they blame Tech.

At the same time, companies want to do more with their data and they need technology to do so. They know they need better data, but they think that the latest technology, be it an enterprise system, a vendor-hosted application, a data warehouse, software as a service, data lakes, a master data management or data governance tool, or cloud-based hosting will somehow correct previously-erred

---

[37] See, for example, W. Edwards Deming, Out of the Crisis, MIT Press, 2000 http://www.amazon.com/Out-Crisis-W-Edwards-Deming/dp/0262541157/.

data and ensure quality going forward. It just doesn't happen this way. Even worse, a mistaken confidence in new technologies distracts companies from placing responsibility for data where it belongs. Companies make this mistake over and over. And blame Tech.

Indeed, new technologies can exacerbate data quality issues. Obviously a new application that helps solve a nagging business problem is all to the good. But today most purchased systems and applications come fully-equipped with their own data structures and data definitions. This is exactly counter to the getting in front approach, which demands that the business, not Tech and certainly not an external vendor, assume responsibility to define data. The result is that the data quite don't line up, new systems to old and exacerbating the "systems don't talk" issue discussed in Chapter 4.

The obvious next step is that Tech sets up a data factory that translates the data back and forth as needed. This is hard work, fraught with error even under the best of circumstances. More systems mean a larger, more complex, and more expensive factory, inevitably creating more errors and leading to more misinterpretations by customers. Not surprisingly, Tech catches the blame. All the while, the sheer growth in data volumes and the pace of technological change continue to explode. Still, companies ask their Tech departments to do more with less.

Tech is not blameless in any of this. It continues to automate broken processes, including other departments' data factories, the history of dismal failures notwithstanding. Tech continues to purchase systems without a moment's thought to how they will fit into a broader

> I sometimes find the Tech department a bit schizophrenic when it comes to data quality. Most readily admit that the business must own the data, that they've been unfairly tasked with too many data efforts that they cannot do well, and their reputations have suffered as a result. Still they can't give data up. Almost like moths drawn to a candle.

data architecture, already an ill-defined and ill-tamed rat's nest. And it continues to build larger, more complex data factories to compensate for its failure in this regard.

At the same time, great data quality programs need great Tech support, for easy-to-navigate data dictionaries, automated measurement and controls, human-to-machine and machine-to-machine interfaces that promote data quality, and so forth. So Tech departments must walk a thin line. They must simultaneously provide solid support (far better than most do currently), and convince their business counterparts that they, not Tech, must take principle responsibility for data quality. Tech must ensure that data translation is done well, insisting that the business delivers clear data definitions. Over the long-term, Tech must get in front in simplifying the data architecture. Finally, Tech must have the courage to "just say no" if business counterparts don't hold up their ends.

**Instructions:**

1. Recognize and deal with the organizational and political realities you face in data space. I've discussed these realities above.
2. Take responsibility for storing data safely, securely, and efficiently, as it is created; moving it where it is needed; and delivering it to data customers. Put in place the technological means to do so.
3. Automate well-defined processes to translate data as it moves between data creators, data customers, organizations, applications, and systems.
4. Contribute to the data quality effort in other ways. Automate well-defined processes, controls, measurements, and data dictionaries. Help with tool selection and configure those tools. Design interfaces that promote data quality.
5. Don't take responsibility for data quality. Resist the temptation to automate poorly-defined processes. To the degree you can, help others assume their responsibilities.
6. Use all definitions, especially the common ones, in new systems development going forward. Insist that the chief data architect deliver solid data definitions and clear standards. Do not accept vendors' data definitions unless they align with your own.

7. Then, and only then, take steps to simplify the data architecture.

8. Build the organizational capabilities needed to implement these instructions.

## STORE, MOVE, AND DELIVER DATA SAFELY AND SECURELY

The most important goal of this book is to clarify managerial responsibilities for data quality. I've stressed the moments of data creation and data use. Get those wrong and quality suffers!

But of course there is more. Upon creation, data does not magically store itself safely away, nor does it announce itself, on cue, at the moment of use. It does not secure itself, distinguishing "good guys," with rightful access, from "bad guys," and protect itself from those who wish to steal it. If data creators and data customers bear responsibility for data at select moments, Tech bears responsibility at all other times. This is the blocking and tackling of data management. It is demanding, unappreciated work. Tech must take care of these things, for both the data per se and the associated data definitions.

## AUTOMATE DATA TRANSLATION AS DATA MOVES FROM SYSTEM TO SYSTEM

It bears repeating that Tech must not take responsibility for data creation. At the same time, one of Tech's roles is to automate well-defined processes, including translating data from the language of one system or application as it

> Tech does, of course, create and use some data and data definitions for its own purposes. Clearly it must assume roles of data creators and data customers in these situations.

moves to another. To do so, Tech needs data definitions and any difficult translation logic. In this respect Tech is a customer, like any other data customer and it should follow the instructions of Chapter 3.

Failing to do so, Tech may be left with poor definitions and no translation logic—a recipe for disaster. I recommend that Tech be circumspect here. Tech may be capable of developing translation logic, if it has clear data definitions. But I don't see how it can proceed without these.

> Examples of such translation include converting money from one currency in a local system to another in a global system; converting a "contact" in a Marketing system to a "prospect" in a Sales system; and converting a "drawing" in a CAD system to "specs" in a Manufacturing system.

The more detailed instructions under these circumstances are:

1. Help the chief data architect provide you the definitions you need.
2. If there is no chief data architect, work with systems providers and integrators, and others to obtain them. And however you obtain them, make sure you understand them.
3. Document the translation logic and review it with the chief data architect. Alternatively, review the logic with those on both ends of the translation, i.e., the original data creator and customer.
4. With these documents, consider yourself an "enabled data creator." So follow the instructions of Chapter 4, including those on measurement and control.

## CONTRIBUTE TO THE DQ EFFORT

Tech should treat DQ teams, embedded data managers, and data creators as customers. These people have enormous (and growing) needs for technology to make measurements, automate controls, promulgate data definitions, and lock in process improvements. They need help in selecting the best tools and of course Tech must install, configure, and maintain those tools.

I'll cite two other examples of the sorts of contributions Tech can make. Not too long ago, one filled in a web-based form and hit "send." Sometime later, you might get an email, advising that "we still need your address," because evidently you hadn't put it in. The email message is an attempt at a control, one that most recipients ignored.

A better control, which most web-sites employ now, involves checking the form as people enter the data. If some is missing, the site stops them from going to the next part of the form and highlights the missing data. A far better control!

A second example involves a human-to-computer interface that makes it easier for people to enter and interpret data. Thus a great feature is what I call the "instant data dictionary." When a data customer positions his or her mouse over a term, its definition pops up in a little window. No searching around!

## DON'T TAKE OVERALL RESPONSIBILITY FOR DATA QUALITY

Since Tech does not own a broken business process, it cannot fix it. Since Tech doesn't own an important decision, it cannot tell the decision-maker what data is most critical. Since Tech doesn't speak the same language as business people, it cannot dictate what business terms mean. Nor can Tech hold data creators and data customers accountable for following the instructions called for herein.

Most of the hard work of data quality management cannot be performed by Tech nor automated by technology. Indeed, Tech is singularly ill-positioned to lead a data quality effort. Too many people and companies assume otherwise.

Worse, too many Tech departments get tagged with data quality. In some cases, a subtle dynamic lies at the root of the misassignment. Data quality enters the conversation while some new system is under development. Its users have naturally assumed its data will be better than the old system's. If not, why go to the new system? Interestingly, no one points out that simply moving bad data from an old system to a new one can't improve quality.

For its part, Tech recognizes that bad data will imperil acceptance of its new system. With a big development project in jeopardy, Tech decides it must do whatever it can to clean up data. So it creates a data factory, though this one is expensive and not so easily hidden. And in so doing, Tech gets tagged with data quality. While the details differ, the underlying dynamic is exactly the same as with the rising star's assistant in Chapter 2.

As with all hidden data factories, management must get in front of the dynamic. At a minimum, Tech should just say "No. We can't do data quality well" and move on. This instruction also applies to calls to automate a broken process. Tech departments violate this instruction all of the time. I frequently hear two rationalizations:

> *"Data quality is important and, if no one else will address it, then Tech must."*

> *"If we don't address data quality, then our systems will look bad."*

While both rationales seem compelling, they are based on the faulty premise that Tech can address data quality. It takes courage to admit you can't, but displaying that courage beats the alternative!

More proactively, Tech must do a better job recognizing the effort required from its business counterparts if its projects are to succeed. It must be completely transparent about the people, time, and costs these efforts require and build them into its development plans. And it must engage early on to secure those resources.

Finally, and most proactively of all, senior Tech management should work with its business counterparts to put a proper data quality program in place.

## USE BUSINESS DATA DEFINITIONS IN SYSTEMS DEVELOPMENT

To open this chapter, I noted that Tech gets tagged with the "systems don't talk" issue and the reduced quality that comes with it. In Chapter 4, I showed that the root of the problem lies in language and can only be resolved by the business. I also laid out several instructions for doing so. The last instruction however, "Use all definitions, especially the common ones, in new systems development going forward" is more properly directed at Tech. Doing so helps ensures that new systems faithfully represent the language employed by their users, in turn helping data customers know what the data mean.

Now to be clear, this instruction is not "insist that all new systems only use pre-existing data definitions." That is far too rigid. But do understand, early on, the definitions a potential new system will employ, how closely aligned the system's definitions are to your own data definitions, and what it will take to translate between the two.

## REDUCE DATA TRANSLATION BY SIMPLIFYING THE DATA ARCHITECTURE

Data translation is necessary because data customers need data in the form and in the applications where they can best use it. At the same time, translation is fraught, contributing errors and leading customers to misinterpret data. Instructions so far aim to ensure that translation is done properly. When possible, Tech departments should also reduce the number of required translations.

Doing so depends on eschewing "system to system" translations, in favor of an approach that makes reference to common definitions. Figure 8.1 illustrates the basic idea.

To be clear, common data definitions are necessary, but not sufficient.[38] Tech must also:

1. Shift its development focus from one that concentrates solely on providing functionality, to one that also embraces "fit" of systems with one and other.

---

[38] Collectively, I call these instructions and those for developing data definitions the "design for fit" approach.

2. Use these common data definitions along with a conceptual data model, and ensure that all future systems (including purchased systems) adhere to it.
3. To the degree possible, separate data from application and system.
4. Acquire the skills needed to execute these steps. A conceptual data modeler and systems engineers are also essential.

**Figure 8.1 Common data definitions can simplify data architecture by reducing the number of interfaces needed between systems.**

Without common data definitions, there are n*(n-1) translations needed between n systems and a new one requires 2n more translations

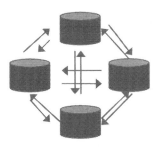

With common data definitions, only 2n translations needed between n systems and a new one requires only 2 more translations

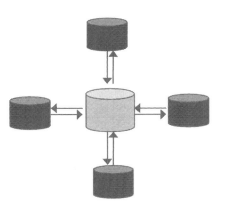

A generation ago, a bedrock principle in corporate computer departments was the separation of data from application, taking the simplified architecture of Figure 8.1 still further. With respect to data quality, decoupling the two had several advantages:

1. It made it easier to build and maintain applications, without disturbing the data.
2. It made it easier to add to and change the data, without disturbing the application.
3. It facilitated data sharing—several applications could use the same data.
4. It minimized error-prone (more below), time-consuming, and costly work of moving data around and translating it.

Embrace this principle to the degree you can, even if full adherence is not possible.

## Put in Place a Powerful Team to Support Data Quality

Figure 8.2 depicts the team needed to carry out these instructions. Except for the Business Customer Team (which serves exactly the same role as a data creator's Customer Team), the roles line up with the sections above. More and more Tech departments are also federating, with some groups aligning more closely with day-in, day-out work and business functions and dedication to infrastructure. With the possible exception of the Architecture Team, these roles should line up as close to DQ Teams, data customers, and data creators as possible.

Throughout this book I've stressed the importance of communications among all who touch data. Without it, too many things go wrong. And without a dedicated role, people and organizations revert into their silos. In many respects, the instruction to assign a Business Customer Team is no different than a data creator assigning a Customer Team. But I find this work is much more difficult for Tech. I see plenty of reasons—the tech community (not surprisingly) views the work as non-technical, there are no career paths, and many in the Tech community are introverts, more comfortable at their keyboards than in a face-to-face meeting with customers.

Figure 8.2 Organization structure for tech data quality team.

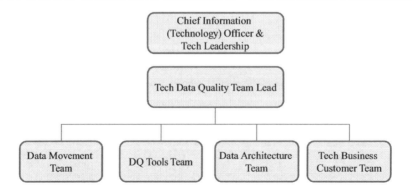

I have no easy solutions, though every technologist who establishes an ongoing dialogue with his or her business counterparts is glad he or she did!

## In Summary

For too long, Tech has either taken or been given primary responsibility for data quality. But Tech is neither a major data creator nor data customer, so this responsibility is misplaced. Tech must help get these roles properly established.

Further, excellent data quality programs require excellent Tech support, particularly as they scale up. Much detailed work is needed and Tech's first role is to do it well. Over the longer term, Tech can make an enormous contribution if it simplifies the data architecture. It should only take on that work if its business counterparts hold up their end in developing and standardizing business terminology/data definitions. Finally, to do these things, Tech must align more closely with the business, something it has not done well in the past.

# CHAPTER 9
## Data Quality in Practice

This chapter presents two case studies that illustrate the most important points of this book as they play out, often messily, in practice. Both feature the getting-in-front approach and the roles of data customers, data creators, a provocateur to get the ball rolling, quality managers and embedded data managers to keep the work moving, and leaders to make the approach and roles standard. The first case, describes AT&T's work to improve financial performance and predictability for access billing. I've related technical aspects of the work before[39] —here of course the focus is on the "who did what." The second case describes Aera Energy's work to develop common data definitions. I've also told some of the Aera story before.[40] These cases have stood the test of time. Others would do well to emulate them.

## IMPROVING ACCESS BILL QUALITY AT AT&T

This case study picks up with Bob Pautke, manager of Access Financial Assurance, looking for better statistical tools to improve his team's work. This is in the late 1980s, in the heady days after AT&T and local telephone companies had split apart. AT&T ran the long distance network, the telephone companies provided local service and "access" to long distance networks. In a typical call, the caller, say in New Jersey, dials her son in another state, say Colorado. The local New Jersey telephone company (e.g., telco) delivers her call to AT&T, which takes the

---

[39] Redman, Thomas C., "Improve Data Quality for Competitive Advantage, *Sloan Management Review*, Winter, 1995, p. 95-107.

[40] See Chapter 8 of *Data Driven*.

call to Colorado. There, the local Colorado telco picks up the call and delivers the call to her son. The telco portions of the call are the aforementioned "access."

Access was under enormous scrutiny. AT&T simply could not function if it couldn't connect to customers. Access, at over $15B/year, was AT&T's largest expense. It was a technical challenge and an important source of revenue to telcos. Further, the whole idea of splitting AT&T and the telcos in the first place was to ensure that AT&T competitors had fair access to customers. So access garnered enormous political, judicial, and regulatory attention.

Divestiture rolled out quickly—the massive task involved setting up the telcos, splitting up hundreds of thousands of employees and plant and equipment worth over a $100 billion, and getting up and running. Not surprisingly, providing service was the number one priority, and billing for those services a distant second (Note: from my perspective, billing was a secondary objective for both AT&T and other telephone companies prior to divestiture as well. They were, after all, regulated monopolies, with, surprisingly to some, strong service cultures. While not stated, the attitude seemed to me to be, "Provide high-quality service first, worry about collecting the money later").

With a lot of money at stake, AT&T developed a bill verification and claims process. When it received an invoice for access, AT&T paid the bill. In parallel, it developed a "predicted bill," using its own sources, and compared it with the original bill. If the discrepancy was large and in the telco's favor, AT&T filed a claim for the perceived overbilling. If the telco agreed, it would rebate the difference. If it disagreed, the telco would reject the claim, providing additional evidence to support its rejection. The telco could even file "counterclaims" if, for example, it found evidence of errors in its original billing in AT&T's favor. Finally, there were plenty of original bills, claims, and counterclaims for which the evidence was mixed. In some cases, AT&T and the telco lumped them together and reached a settlement.

Figure 9.1 depicts the end-to-end process. Overall, bill verification was time-consuming, expensive and yielded uncertain results. Still, it was easy enough to justify: both sides were simply protecting their interests.

**Figure 9.1 Access Bill Verification at AT&T.**

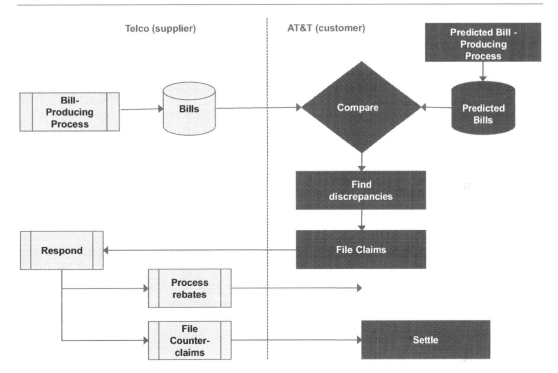

## Improve bill verification

The obvious step to improve financial performance is to improve the predicted bill. Better predicted bills meant better claims, in turn leading to more rebates. Of course, better predicted bills required better data, so from time to time AT&T would cleanse its own data. For their part, telcos also saw the need for high-quality data and so conducted their own clean-ups.

> Bill verification and efforts to clean up data to improve bill verification constitute hidden data factories and it is simple to see how easy it is to justify them.

It is important to note that in some ways bill verification "worked." The number and dollar value of claims decreased. Rebates far exceeded the cost of obtaining them. And many in AT&T came to view rebates as "revenue." After all, money coming in is important, no matter what the source.

Pautke was responsible for so-called "special access," those involving private lines (a private line connects a single customer, often a large business that needs lots of service, to the telephone network). Though he couldn't articulate it well, Pautke was dissatisfied. In particular, the private line business is dynamic: existing customers need more services, new customers

> Provocateurs are important for many reasons—they may see the hidden data factory when others don't, they may be dissatisfied with results, or they may simply wonder why something costs so darn much. What distinguished them is that they have the courage to speak up and push on. Companies are in their debt!

need new services, businesses set up new locations, and all may need new features. A sort of dynamic equilibrium evolved—new issues were created each month, some were resolved, some lumped together and settled.

The statistical tools Pautke sought aimed to help him understand these issues more deeply. He reached out to his director, Scott Williamson, who in turn, reached out to me, at the Bell Laboratories Quality Assurance Center. Earlier I had studied network performance and was looking to try out statistical process control on the operation of the network. Young Huh, a specialist in product reliability, and later others, joined me in assisting Pautke.

The problem Pautke posed was improving predicted bills. The three of us quickly agreed on a different approach. Rather than figuring out better ways to clean up the data needed to create a predicted bill, we should focus on the process that created the data.

## Traction

Interestingly, no one understood this process in any detail. People knew how systems interconnected, but they did not know what happened to the data. To find out, Pautke and his team conducted a small tracking study. To do so, they picked 20 new service orders and then followed the data involved at each step. Figure 9.2 depicts a portion of one tracked record. Note four anomalies, in red italics. The first two changes (from XYZ.1234 to *XYZ-1234* and from 1 to *A*) involved re-formatting the data during step B. They discovered a number of small changes like this as they looked through the data. Some were annoying, but none appeared to impact invoices. The other two changes noted in Figure 9.2, were more substantial. The billing number and office numbers changed mid-process. These changed the meaning in the data and impacted the invoice. Pautke and his team did not expect to see such changes as the data winded its way along.

Figure 9.2 A portion of a tracked record. The process features five steps and the table features four, of dozens, of data attributes. Thus the billing code for this item of work, at step A is "1." Finally, the entries in red represent unexpected changes in the data record.

| Attribute | Step of Process | | | | |
|---|---|---|---|---|---|
| | **A** | **B** | **C** | **D** | **E** |
| **Name** | XYZ.1234 | *XYZ-1234* | XYZ-1234 | XYZ-1234 | XYZ-1234 |
| **Billing Number** | | | 272-791-2424 | *272-791-9100* | 272-791-9100 |
| **Bill Code** | 1 | *A* | A | A | A |
| **Office** | 408727 | 408727 | 408727 | *408927* | *408970* |
| **...** | | | | | |

Further, for each of the 20 new service orders, Pautke and his team found something that just didn't look right. At this point no one fully understood the implications. Many people were dismissive. After all, what can you prove with 20 records? So Pautke and his team did not yet have real traction.

Williamson, the most senior AT&T manager, didn't fully understand the implications either. But he knew early results could not be ignored and he made sure that Pautke and his Bell Labs support team had the political cover and resources to push on.

Note that, having found something that troubled him, Pautke had not just spoken up, he had followed up, key to being a provocateur.

To gain traction, Pautke and his team had to demonstrate that their approach was a valid alternative. They did so by automating their tracking efforts to increase numbers and looking for patterns in the results.

They started using time series and Pareto plots to gain insights into such questions. Figure 9.3 removed any doubt that the process performed extremely poorly. On average, only 40 percent of the data records made it all of the way through without error.

Figure 9.3 Predicted bill process performance, weeks 1-10.

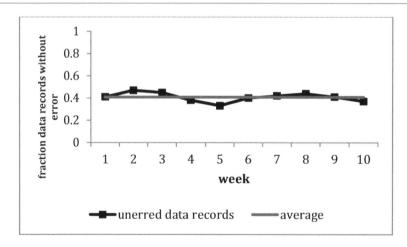

They also sought to determine where errors occurred by making dozens of plots. Many, such as Figure 9.4, yielded no particular insight. But Figure 9.5 proved more fruitful. It shows that the vast majority of problems occurred in a relatively few attributes.

Figure 9.4 Process performance by service type, weeks 1-10.

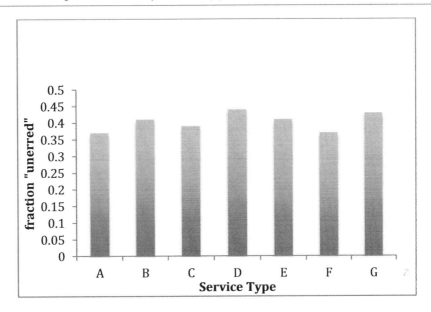

Figure 9.5 Process performance by attribute, weeks 1-10.

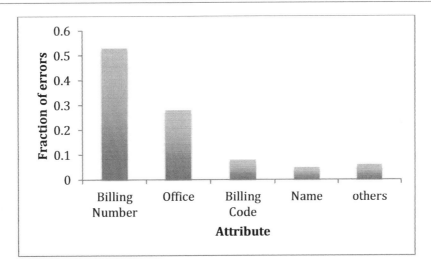

Pautke and his team made many such plots. The one that proved most insightful was Figure 9.6, which showed that the vast majority of problems occurred on the interfaces between steps C and D. A few also occurred between steps D and E, but almost none between steps A and B and B and C.

Figure 9.6 Interfaces where errors occur, all attributes, weeks 1-10.

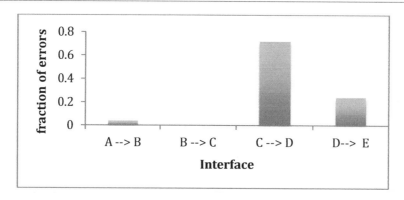

Next, combining the insight from Figure 9.6 with that revealed in Figure 9.5, they were able to precisely identify exactly where the problems occurred (Figure 9.7). This is critical! Rather than tens of thousands (maybe hundreds of thousands) of individual issues that had to be addressed one at a time, it became clear that eliminating a relatively few root causes would dramatically improve data quality.

Figure 9.7 Process performance by interface and attribute, weeks 1-10.

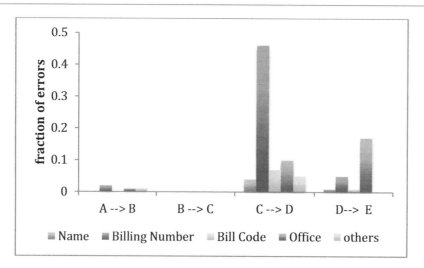

Pautke spent an inordinate amount of time explaining these results. As he did so, a critical mass of managers grew dissatisfied with bill verification. The "claims are revenue" mantra was replaced with a simple analogy to a gold mine. In the analogy, one party seeded a mine with the second party's gold. The second party used its best technology and other means to recover that gold. But it could hardly count that gold as revenue. There was no way to come out ahead. Even if the second party recovered all its gold, it had expended enormous time and energy to do so.

Finally, Pautke had traction!

### First real results

Traction aside, Pautke had not yet achieved a consensus on what to do next. Some opined that if AT&T could create an extremely high-quality predicted bill, that it ought to do away with telephone company billing (and AT&T bill verification) altogether. Others thought it more appropriate to share the tracking technique with telephone companies and help/train/insist/demand that they find and eliminate the root causes in their processes. Discussions continued for months and it is easy to see them as a bureaucratic waste of time. That conclusion misses the point—these discussions socialized a new technology and a new approach with hundreds of people.

As fate would have it, Pautke was based in Cincinnati, and AT&T and Cincinnati Bell (CB) shared a building. Many people were former colleagues and personal friends. The lunchtime discussion one day between Pautke and Cori Rothenbach turned to billing and he relayed his excitement about data tracking and growing frustration with bill verification. Rothenbach was just as frustrated. She found AT&T a difficult partner (perhaps putting it kindly!), sending far too much corrupt data and causing extra effort to set up and bill for CB services. At the same time, she was confident that CB's data was outstanding.

Rothenbach talked to others in CB and, within a week or two, AT&T and CB agreed to track data across company lines.

A critical moment occurred during an early discussion. Pautke had stated that all AT&T wanted was a "timely and accurate bill." The response from the Cincinnati Bell people stunned him: "You know Bob, we don't come in every morning thinking of ways to foul you up. What exactly do you mean by 'timely and accurate?'"

Pautke knew in an instant! Rather than explaining what it wanted, AT&T had plunged headlong into bill verification. It had failed in its responsibilities as a customer and it had only itself to blame for bad data coming from Cincinnati Bell. This subtle observation is extremely important and I'll have more to say about it in a moment.

> I cannot overemphasize the need for communications in data quality management. A major contributing factor in every data quality program I've work on was the data creators simply did not understand what data creators required. And, as Pautke found, data customers have only themselves to blame if they've not explained their needs to data creators.

To its credit, Cincinnati Bell only required a few tracked records to see that its data was not perfect. With its strong service ethic, this was simply unacceptable. AT&T, for its part, acknowledged CB's complaints about its data.

So the two companies worked together, across company lines, tracking new customer orders from the receipt, through provisioning, through billing. They did find some errors that were solely one or the other's fault, but most occurred on interfaces between the companies, the most important of which is between steps C and D in the prior discussion. At a deeper level, the real root cause was poor communication of each company's needs as data crossed these interfaces. Defining those needs in full detail was the key to fixing the interfaces, in turn eliminating most billing errors.

## Rollout

Even with the success of data tracking and the CB work, few AT&T managers thought it feasible to eliminate bill verification. After all, CB is a small company, not likely to impress the others. There was plenty of internal debate and discussion, but again no consensus on next steps emerged.

In another twist of fate, Scott Williamson, so influential in getting the work started and nurturing it along, took early retirement. His replacement, Monica Mehan, came from a different part of the company and had no investment in any aspect of the work. As she learned about her new organization, she found data tracking to be cool and the CB trial intriguing. Conversely, bill verification held no appeal. She thought the only responsible course involved trying to replicate the CB work with all telcos and she charged one of her lieutenants, John Tomka, with getting on with it.

> Mehan's decisiveness and sense of urgency were essential. As I noted earlier, data quality programs go as far and as fast as the senior leader perceived to be leading the effort demands. If Pautke had poked the bear, now the bear arose from its slumber.

For the new approach to work, other telcos would have to invest in data tracking and become willing partners. But would they do so? After all, telcos were monopoly providers, given, in the eyes of some, short shrift at divestiture. What was in it for them?

In one respect the CB trial was more prescient than one could have expected. Each telco hated the entire bill verification and claims process just as much as CB. To them, it was an expense, and a huge, unpredictable one at that. Actually, it was two expenses—the monies they returned to AT&T and the expense of responding to claims. They incurred this second expense even when an AT&T claim was wrong. Thus, at a high level, telco and AT&T interests aligned. Still high-level alignment and a clear way forward are two different things. Developing that clear way forward required a bit more work.

There are two types of billing errors: overcharges, where the telco bill is too high, and undercharges, where it is too low. To protect its financial interests, AT&T sought to eliminate overcharges; conversely, the telco sought to eliminate undercharges. Senior managers on both sides came to realize a simple reality: The only way to turn off bill verification was for each to recognize the other's interests—and drive both overcharges and undercharges to zero.

Two specific measures were developed to crystallize these ideas:

- **Risk**. The total dollars at risk to either company, estimated as the sum of overcharges and undercharges.
- **Consequence**. The difference between overcharges and undercharges and represents the amount of money that should change hands.

To illustrate the points, consider two situations:

A: Overcharges = $1,000; Undercharges = $500

B: Overcharges = $2,000; Undercharges = $1,750.

Then the statistics work as:

A: Risk = $1,500; Consequence = $500

B: Risk = $3,750; Consequence = $250.

It's clear enough that case B is better in the short term—fewer dollars change hands. At the same time, case A portends a better long-term future—there are considerably fewer dollars to worry about. The simple insight that both the short terms and long terms mattered crystallized a direction: Continue bill verification to keep the consequence low (serving companies' financial interests) while simultaneously work together to drive risk to zero. Then turn off bill verification.

Tomka, Pautke and their teams wrapped up these ideas in a vision they labeled Future Optimal State or FOS. A claimless environment, in which companies trusted one another, the risk was low (if risk is low, then consequence must be low), and bill verification was no longer needed.

Earlier I noted that Pautke came to realize that AT&T was partly to blame for its access billing problems. Slowly, others in AT&T came to realize this as well. Before the work began, any manager asked, "Who's to blame for telco billing issues?"

would reply, "The telco!" without batting an eye. People came to realize that such thinking was incomplete, maybe even wrong. The practical reality is that when one party (e.g., a data customer) checks the data provided by a second party (e.g., a data creator), it tacitly assumes responsibility for the quality of that party's data. Even if needed in the short term, this is almost always a bad idea in the long term. AT&T came to realize that it had baked in a bad idea with bill verification.

AT&T had not been a good customer either. It wasn't just CB that didn't understand what AT&T meant by a "timely and accurate bill," no telco did either (in retrospect, judging from the effort required to document that seemingly simple concept, I suspect that AT&T didn't know either).

The FOS vision required both AT&T (as the customer) and telcos (as the creators) to assume their rightful roles. Thus AT&T would:

- Define exactly what it wanted and help the telco understand.
- Provide the telco with correct data so it would provision and bill correctly.
- Replace bill verification with supplier management.

And the telco would:

- Assume full responsibility for bill accuracy.
- Provide evidence that bills were correct.
- Identify and eliminate root causes of error as quickly as possible.

Tomka's next step was to build the organizational structure needed to achieve FOS. He put the following in place:

- A FOS Core Team, made up solely of AT&T people, responsible for the detailed definition of the FOS program, clarifying AT&T requirements, certifying that FOS objectives had been achieved, and overall program management.
- Implementation teams, made up (largely) of telco employees, charged with translating AT&T requirements into a specific plan and implementing that plan. Each implementation team was given latitude in meeting AT&T

requirements and a core team member stuck close, to answer questions and help make day-to-day decisions.

- One steering committee per telco, composed of a core team member, the

> The core team serves as the data quality team, the implementation team as embedded data managers, and the steering committees as leadership.

leader of the implementation team, and senior managers from both sides. These teams met quarterly and bore ultimate responsibility for successful implementation.

The work proceeded at a steady pace. Figure 9.8 depicts key features of the new end-to-end cross-company process. Random samples of customer orders were tracked across company lines, bill-impacting issues noted, estimates of risk and consequence created and likely root causes called out. Dozens, maybe hundreds of issues came up. As with CB, most errors occurred on the interfaces of departments within companies or between companies. Almost all were relatively easy to address. Every single implementation team reduced risk by 90 percent with a few months of serious work.

Within two years, bill verification was turned off for all large telcos. Billing errors were reduced by 98 percent and both the phone companies and AT&T saved tens of millions per year. The unquantified, and probably unquantifiable, benefits may be even greater. Frank Ianna, then head of AT&T's Network Operations Division, explained it to me this way, "In the past I'd get month-end summaries about three weeks after the end of each month. But they didn't end anything, because results could change dramatically. For example, I couldn't feel comfortable with January results until August. It's no way to run the business. Don't get me wrong. I do appreciate the improvements to the bottom line. But being able to run the business is worth even more."

As this case illustrates, improving data quality can be truly transformative in its own right.

Finally, improving data quality changed everything, for everyone involved. Jobs were lost and every job was very different after! Just compare Figures 9.1 and 9.8. The new work looks nothing like the old.

Figure 9.8 New access financial assurance process.

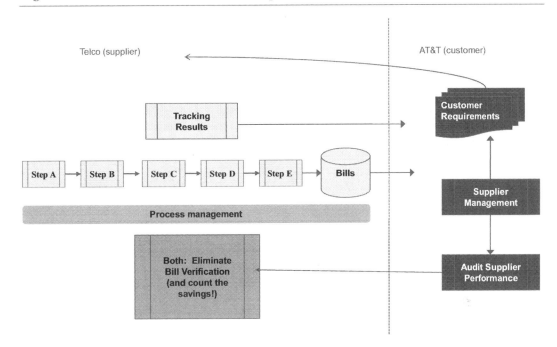

## DATA DEFINITIONS THAT STAND THE TEST OF TIME AT AERA ENERGY

While the AT&T example focuses on the quality of data values, this one focuses on data definitions, so important if data customers are to understand what the data means.

The basic roles are no less relevant for metadata. In particular, creating a data definition is similar to creating a data value and data customers need both to use data effectively. One company that's done terrific work to define its most important data, keep those definitions current, and add new ones as needed is Aera Energy. Based in Bakersfield, Aera is an oil and gas company, focused on onshore and offshore exploration and production assets formerly operated by Shell and Mobil in California.

The key players include Gene Voiland, then Aera Chief Executive; David Walker, CIO; Bob Palermo, chief architect; Lwanga Yonke, information process owner; Marie Davis, Aera's data architect; Dave Hay, a consultant in data modeling; and a network of 30 data stewards. Unlike most other companies, Aera and its executives recognized the importance of both data and process. So they defined 11 key processes, set on top of the usual business unit structure. "Manage information" was set squarely in the middle of the process structure, both feeding and depending on the other 10. Here Voiland, Walker, and Palermo play the leadership roles, Yonke data quality management, Davis and Hay provide technical expertise, and the data stewards play the role of embedded data managers. Interestingly, the data stewards played dual roles, amplifying the voice of the data customer and participating in the actual creation of data definitions. These stewards were appointed by the process owners and typically were business professionals.

Many people have no appreciation for all of the fuss about data definitions. After all, doesn't everyone have access to a dictionary? But it turns out that

> Recall that most people are both data customers and data creators. Embedding data managers enables them to help with both roles.

everyday business language takes on meanings that go far beyond the dictionary. Terms can be vague and confusing—a term can follow one definition in one situation and quite another in a different situation. In Aera's case, one term that is obviously important is "well" as in oil well. Clearly, it is a term that people in the oil business use every day. But what exactly is a "well"?

- *Is it a "hole in the ground"?*

- *Is it a "hole in the ground from which oil is being extracted"? If so, what is a "hole in the ground that has been capped off"?*
- *What if, below ground level, a spur is drilled off the original hole, forming an inverted "Y." One well or two?*
- *What if, through the same hole, two distinct subsurface oil zones are being produced, each one with its own production and fluid measurement equipment? How many wells now?*

Imagine the confusion that will result when two people employ different definitions. Then each will give different answers to that most basic of questions, "How many wells do we have?" These complications grow as applications exchange data.

The job of getting the right definitions involved two steps. The first, led by Palermo, consisted primarily of identifying 53 important terms (such as "well") and sketching initial definitions. The second step, led by Yonke, was aimed at getting agreement on the meanings of these terms, crystallizing them into a conceptual data model, and developing logical data models to support new computer applications.

To be clear, all important business terms require clear definition. These must be captured and made available via a data dictionary. But not all terms require standardization. A much smaller number (53 in Aera's case) will suffice.

Note that Yonke's job was to manage the process, not develop specific definitions. Since the process spans the entire company, the job may be likened to herding cats. As he pointed out, "It's a challenge to manage a process in which no one reports directly to you. You have to lead through influence and well-defined systems. While I was responsible for the overall process, the stewards were responsible for the individual results."

It is important to recognize that it takes time to develop and agree upon good data definitions (in contrast, processes such as those Pautke worked on creating vast quantities of data values). But spending the time is worth the effort. Good data definitions have long shelf lives, since they cut to the heart of the company. They should outlast systems, reorganizations, even entire generations. Davis noted "As we worked through the process, individual teams came to realize that they had to do more than just represent the interests of their own business units. They had to do what was right for everyone in Aera. That took time. It also helped us appreciate each other's perspectives and contributions a lot more."

While creating solid data definitions (and of course maintaining them) is worth the time and effort, it is difficult to estimate return on investment. Still, Aera's sustained implementation has yielded a wide array of benefits. Palermo noted "One of our goals was to enable engineers to spend more time on engineering analysis and decision-making, and less on data management. On that score we can show that we've doubled the productivity of most of these critical people."

## In Summary

What's most striking to me about AT&T's and Aera's work and results is not how great they are, but how utterly typical they are. In the diffusion of the getting in front approach and the roles and methods that support it, these two companies make up the bleeding edge. Others, in telecommunications, oil and gas, retail, and finance have followed and achieved similar results. In contrast to the "bleeding edge," these comprise the "leading edge." They've proven that the approach works. And pays! Similar results are available to all who devote serious effort to the task.

# CHAPTER 10
## Advancing Data Quality

A fair-minded reader, scanning this book the first time, may well react in horror! "We don't have anything like this. No provocateurs, no embedded data managers, no leadership. People don't recognize themselves as data creators and customers. Indeed, we have a data quality team. But it is buried in Tech and is completely ineffective."

Horrified or not, you only have three choices when it comes to the instructions laid out in this book: You can ignore them, you can start to work on them,

> It should be no surprise that today's organizations are unfit for data—they were designed for a different time. They were perfectly suited for industrialization and concepts such as division of labor that came with it. These organizations have become enormously effective! So let's not cast them aside lightly. At the same time, recognize that they are not well-suited to data—they've led to silos that get in the way of data sharing and make the sorts of customer-with-creator conversations more difficult, they've led to incorrectly assigning the data to IT, and they've made it more difficult to unleash the power of data. Putting the people and structures called for here and following these instructions is a powerful step in the right direction.

or you can try something different. Ignoring them is risky and it gets riskier every day. Data is changing everything, as no less an authority on strategy and competition than Michael Porter[41] observed, "…All this has major implications for the classic organizational structure of manufacturers. What is under way is

---

[41] Michael Porter and James Heppelmann, "How Smart, Connected Products Are Transforming Companies," *Harvard Business Review*, October 2015. I also urge readers to read "How Smart, Connected Products Are Transforming Companies," *Harvard Business Review*, November 2014, by the same authors.

perhaps the most substantial change in the manufacturing firm since the second Industrial Revolution, more than a century ago." And that is only manufacturers! You just can't participate with bad data.

If you wish try something different, I encourage you to do so. We need a lot of innovation in this space!

That said, consider giving the getting in front approach and these instructions a solid try. Anyone can be a provocateur, so start with instructions that appeal the most, and learn as you go. If you're low in the organizational hierarchy, start with something you can control. If you're higher up, seed as many data quality initiatives as you can!

This book features dozens, maybe hundreds, of instructions. But let's not make this any more complicated than it needs to be. Which are most important? I nominate the following five, because they include everyone. Indeed, an entire company can take them as rallying cry:

1. Grow increasingly intolerant of bad data, the hidden data factories and other bad results it engenders.
2. Adopt the "get in front on data quality" philosophy, focusing on creating data, and data definitions, correctly the first time. More than a simple philosophy, getting in front on data quality represents a profound cultural shift.
3. Data customers and data creators must play the most important roles— customers must define what's most important, and creators must focus on delivering that most important data. Recognize that each of us is both a customer and creator, often simultaneously.
4. Build a federated organization for data quality, featuring embedded data managers who help customers and creators in their roles; data quality managers, who help them connect; leadership, which must bear the mantle of ensuring the new philosophy is followed; and Tech, which builds the supporting infrastructure.
5. No matter who you are, let your inner data provocateur out.

This appendix is aimed at senior decision makers and data scientists whose needs for quality data are extremely stringent. A decision or analysis sent in the wrong direction due to bad data is far more costly than the operational expenses contemplated by the rule of ten. At the same time, you may have to deal with wholly new data that, when combined with existing data, could offer potentially game-changing insights. But there isn't a clear indication whether this new information can be trusted. How should you proceed?

There is, of course, no simple answer. While many are skeptical of new data (perhaps having been burned) and others embrace it wholeheartedly (perhaps in a headlong rush to establish their credentials as data-driven), I recommend a nuanced approach. For it is highly likely that some data (maybe even most of it) is bad and can't be used, and some is good and should be trusted implicitly. Finally some data is flawed but usable with caution. This data is intriguing as many game-changing insights reside there. So how should you separate the good data from bad?

First, evaluate the data's origins. You can trust data when it is created in accordance with a first-rate data quality program (refer to Chapter 4). Such programs feature clear accountabilities, input controls, and efforts to find and eliminate the root causes of error. You'll not have to opine whether the data are good—data quality statistics will tell you. You'll find a human being who'll be

---

[42] This Appendix is based largely on Thomas Redman, "Can Your Data be Trusted?," October 29, 2015, https://hbr.org/2015/10/can-your-data-be-trusted

happy to explain what you may expect and answer your questions. If the data quality stats look good and the conversation goes well, trust this data. Please note that this is the "gold standard" against which other steps below indicators should be calibrated.

Second, make your own assessment. Much, perhaps most, data will not meet the gold standard, so adopt a more cautious attitude. Make sure you know where the data was created and how it is defined, not just how your data scientist accessed it. It is easy to be misled by a casual, "We took them from our cloud-based data warehouse, which employs the latest technology," and completely miss the fact that the data was created in a dubious public forum. Figure out which organization created the data. Then dig deeper: What do colleagues advise about this organization and data? Does it have a good or poor reputation for quality? What do others say on social media? Do some research both inside and outside your organization.

At the same time, develop your own data quality statistics, possibly using the Friday Afternoon Measurement described in Chapter 2. If you see only a little red, say less than 5% of records with an obvious error, you can use this data with caution. Look too at patterns of the errors. If, for example, there are twenty-five total errors, twenty-four of which occur in one data attribute, eliminate that attribute going forward. But the rest of the data looks pretty good—use it with caution.

Third, clean the data. In this context, I think of data cleaning as on three levels: rinse, wash, and scrub. Rinse replaces obvious errors with "missing value" or corrects them if doing so is very easy; scrub involves deep study, even making corrections one-at-a-time, by hand, if necessary; and wash occupies a middle ground. Even if time is short, scrub a small random sample (say 1000 records), making them as pristine as you possibly can. Your goal is to arrive at a sample of data you know you can trust. Employ all possible means of scrubbing and be ruthless! Eliminate erred data records and data elements that you cannot correct, and mark data as "uncertain" when applicable.

When you are done, take a hard look. When the scrubbing has gone really well (and you'll know it if it does), you've created a dataset that rates high on the trustworthy-scale. Use these data going forward.

Sometimes the scrubbing is less satisfying. If you've done the best you can, but still feel uncertain, put these data in the "use with caution" category. If the scrubbing goes poorly – for example, too much data just looks wrong and you can't make corrections – you must rate this data, and all like it, as untrustworthy. The sample strongly suggests none of this data should be used to inform your decision.

After the initial scrub, move on to the second cleaning exercise: washing the remaining data that was not in the scrubbing sample. This step should be performed by a truly competent data scientist. Since scrubbing can be a time-consuming, manual process, the wash allows you to make corrections using more automatic processes. For example, one wash technique involves statistical imputation,[43] to replace missing values. Or data scientists may discover algorithms during scrubbing. Put the data where washing goes well in the "use with caution" category.

Figure A.1 summarizes. Once you've identified a set of data that you can trust or use with caution, move on to the next step of integration. Finally, ensure high-quality data integration. Align the data you can trust – or the data that you're moving forward with cautiously – with your existing data. This is difficult, technical work, again only to be performed only by a qualified data scientist. Three tasks must be completed:

- Identification: Verify that the Courtney Smith in one dataset is the same Courtney Smith in others.
- Alignment of units of measure and data definitions: Make sure Courtney's purchases and prices paid, expressed in "pallets" and "dollars" in one set, are aligned with "units" and "euros" in another.

---

[43] https://en.wikipedia.org/wiki/Imputation_(statistics)

- De-duplication: Check that the Courtney Smith record does not appear multiple times in different ways (say as C. Smith or Courtney E. Smith).

Figure A.1 Steps a data scientist or senior decision maker should take to evaluate the trustworthiness of data.

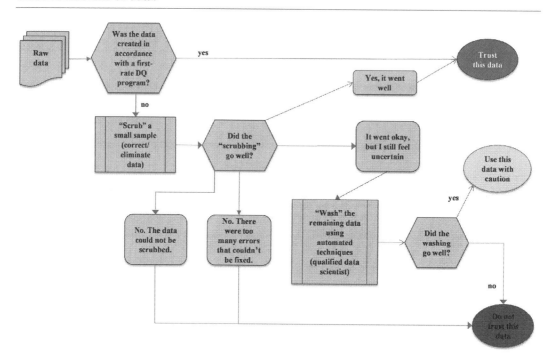

At this point, you're ready to perform whatever analyses you need to guide your decision. Pay particular attention when you get different results based on "use with caution" and "trusted" data. Great insights and, unfortunately, great traps lie here. When a result looks intriguing, isolate the data and repeat the steps above, making more detailed measurements, scrubbing the data, and improving wash routines. As you do so, develop a feel for how deeply you should trust this data.

Taking the steps above will gain you a lot. Understanding where you can trust the data allows you to push the data to its limits. Data doesn't have to be perfect to yield new insights, but you must exercise caution by understanding where the flaws lie, working around errors, cleaning them up, and backing off when the data simply isn't good enough.

# APPENDIX B
## Special Instructions for Automated Measurement, Connected Devices, and the Internet of Things[44]

Many people intuitively think that data created "by computer" or some automated measurement device is far superior to data created by humans. I've not done a careful study, but in my experience this is not the case. Consider the clock on my office file cabinet. This clock synchronizes itself at 1:00 AM every day using a time signal sent out by the National Institute of Standards and Technology, from Fort Collins, Colorado and has an advertised precision in the fraction-of-a-second range. You'd think I could trust it.

Not so. I began to suspect it wasn't perfect one Friday morning when it read 9:32. That meant I was already two minutes late for a meeting that always starts promptly and I had to complete some critical preparation before joining. Stressed, I completed the prep and joined the call, about ten minutes late. But no one else was on. A bit of investigation revealed the clock was running twenty minutes ahead!

So I started a log of clock errors. After some two years, I've noted fifteen separate instances. In one instance the clock was off by three hours. I can rationalize that one—perhaps the clock thought I wanted Pacific time, not Eastern time. But in eight instances, both the time and date were incorrect. In one case it had to be off by about three years. I cannot figure those out. Nor can I figure out the twenty-minute error cited above. Interestingly, this smallest error is the only one that caused any real grief.

---

[44] This Appendix is based on a blog Tom Davenport and I co-authored: "Build Data Quality into the Internet of Things," August 26, 2015, http://blogs.wsj.com/cio/2015/08/26/build-data-quality-into-the-internet-of-things.

A rough estimate of the error rate of my clock is 2.4%,[45] well within the range of the error rate for a typical attribute.

The story provides an apt warning of the dangers in connected devices. The Internet of Things (IoT) is bringing billions of new connected devices into our lives. From Fitbit activity trackers to

> Note that DQ measurements made in Chapter 4 included an entire data record, perhaps 15 -25 attributes and an overall error rate of 30%. My clock is a single attribute only, and so a 2.5% error rate is toward the high-end of the "what's typical" range.

Nest thermostats, to devices embedded in engines and factory machines, excitement is high and the potential is enormous. But as the clock example suggests, it will be much more difficult to achieve that potential if too much IoT data is bad.

Further, bear in mind that clocks are remarkably simple compared to other devices such as accelerometers, locators, and chemical assays. Similar data quality issues can impact all—the Fitbit doesn't count steps on the treadmill (at least in my experience); a device in the electric grid quits working (then mysteriously starts again); the gears in a weather vane fill with sand and compromise the measurement. If I move the scale in my bathroom just a few inches, my measured weight can change by three pounds. Frankly, I find all measurement devices quirky. Don't trust them until you really understand them and they've proven themselves.

Issues associated with data definitions also impact such devices. Individually, most such issues are pretty mundane—a measurement made in yards (English units) but interpreted in meters (metric units) and a misinterpreted relationship

---

[45] Error rate = (number of erred days/number of days I looked at it) = (15/(number of days in 24 months − number of days I traveled)) ≈ (15/(365*2 − 120)) = 15/610 = 2.4%.

between "steps" and "distance walked" (the Fitbit) are good examples. But there are quite literally thousands of such issues, any one of which can trip you up.

Of course, the problem is not just the devices per se. The whole idea of connected devices is that they work together to do things they can't do alone. And here problems grow more acute. For a single device, it is good enough to know whether the units are English or metric. For multiple devices all the units of measure must align to perform even the simplest tasks. It just won't do if your Nest device measures your house temperature in Fahrenheit and transmits it to a utility company that records temperature in Celsius. This means that people and organizations have to agree on how they will measure things.

Standards are the obvious answer, but they take a devilishly long time and much effort. As my sometimes co-author Tom Davenport points out, the development of the EPCGlobal (electronic product code for radio frequency identification) standard took about 15 years. The development of the ANSI X12 standard for electronic data interchange took about 14 years. We don't want to wait that long for anything these days, and standards development could really slow down the penetration of IoT devices.

So how do the instructions of this book apply to the IoT and other connected devices? I've already noted that "bad data is like a virus. There is no telling where it will end up or the damage it will cause." With viruses the basic idea is to try to prevent them in the first place and do all you can to contain them after that.

For data quality and the Internet of Things, preventing the virus starts with excellent design, manufacturing, and installation of the IoT device. Since such devices are typically purchased from another company (a semiconductor manufacturer, for example) you must view yourself as a customer for all the measurements the device will ever make. You must insist the device actually measures what it purports to measure. This implies both specification of the intended measurement and rigorous testing, under both laboratory and real-world conditions, to ensure this actually occurs. Make sure you know what a "step" is and that device actually count them properly.

The specification should spell out operating conditions. Recall that the Fitbit doesn't work so well on the treadmill. The specification should spell out everything you'll need to use the device successfully in practice: what you need to do to install and test it, its expected lifetime, how you'll know when it is time to maintain or replace the device, and so forth.

Insist on two levels of calibration from your device supplier. First, there should be rigorous calibration before the device leaves the factory, and an "on-installation" calibration to ensure that the device works as expected. Second, ongoing calibration is required to make sure the device continues to work properly. Ideally, the on-installation and ongoing calibration routines should be built-in and automated.

To contain bad data, devices should come equipped with so-called "I'm not working right now" and "I'm broken and must be replaced" features, which do exactly what their names suggest.

Finally, you should not expect perfection, particularly with new devices. But you must insist on rapid improvement. So it is critical that either you, or the manufacturer on your behalf, aggregate and analyze the results of all these steps, looking for patterns that suggest improvements. Seek answers to basic questions such as: can the devices really be trusted? Are they lasting as long as expected? What is causing them to fail?

To carry out the above, clarify who in your organization is responsible for the performance of these devices. Ideally, embed the devices, the data they create, and the responsible person within a process.

To conclude, I wish to emphasize that measurement has always been difficult. Not surprisingly, quality has always been a huge issue. The attention scientists have devoted to making trusted measurements underscores the importance of high-quality data to analytics and data science. We should expect no less in business.

**chief data architect.** The owner of the data definition process.

**control.** The managerial act of comparing actual performance to standards and acting on the difference (after Juran).

**data creator.** Any person or process who creates data in the course of his, her, or its work.

**data customer.** Any person or process who uses data to complete his, her, or its work.

**data maestro.** Any individual with broad and deep knowledge of data quality, considerable practical experience, and the gravitas to be a trusted advocate for data quality within his or her organization.

**data provocateur.** Any individual who takes steps to change the course of his work team, department, or company in respect to its management of data quality.

**data quality (aspirational definition).** Exactly the right data in exactly the right place the right time and in the right format to complete an operation, serve a customer, conduct an analysis, craft a plan, make a decision, or set and execute strategy.

**data quality (day-in, day-out definition).** Meeting the most important needs of the most important customers.

**data quality (formal definition).** Data is of high-quality if they are fit for their intended uses (by customers) in operations, analytics, decision-making, and planning. To be fit for use, data must be 'free from defects' (i.e., "right") and 'possess desired features' (i.e., be the "right data").

**data quality team.** Any group charged with improving data quality across a department or corporation.

**embedded data manager.** Any person embedded into a business function whose role involves helping data creators and customers complete their responsibilities in these roles.

**Friday Afternoon Measurement.** A process for measuring data quality that aims to develop a simple, defensible measurement as quickly as possible.

**getting in front/getting in front on data/getting in front on data quality.** An approach, including roles and responsibilities, methods, and tools, that aims to improve data quality by "getting in front" of the issues that cause data to be unfit for use.

**hidden data factory.** Non-value-added work, conducted by individuals, work teams, companies, and departments to make data they need to do their work fit for use.

**process.** Any sequence of work activities, characterized by common inputs and outputs and directed to a common goal.

**process management cycle.** A structured approach for ensuring that a process is managed, end-to-end, with special emphasis (here) on the roles of data creators and data customers.

**proprietary data.** Data owned by a single company, that it can protect and use to create a sustained competitive advantage.

**quality improvement cycle.** A structured approach for putting improvement teams in place and helping them identify and eliminate root causes of error.

**rule of ten.** A rule-of-thumb that advises that it costs ten times as much to complete a simple operation correctly when the data is flawed in any way compared to when they are all fit-for-use.

**supplier management cycle.** A structured approach for working with data suppliers to ensure that one's needs, as a data customer, are met.

**voice of the customer (VoC).** On one level, the Voice of the Customer is a document that summarizes a customer's needs of data from a particular supplier. More abstractly, the idea is that data creators understand who uses data they create, in "the voice of the customer."

30140628R00105

Made in the USA
Lexington, KY
07 February 2019